Year One

Year One

*How Young Professionals (And Their Managers) Can Thrive
in Their First Job After College*

*ALLISON MCWILLIAMS
AND
KATHERINE LAWS*

LIBRARY PARTNERS PRESS
WINSTON-SALEM, NC

ISBN 978-1-61846-120-9

Cover design by Lauren R. Beam

Produced and distributed by

Library Partners Press
ZSR Library
Wake Forest University
1834 Wake Forest Road
Winston-Salem, North Carolina 27106

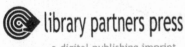

library partners press
a digital publishing imprint

www.librarypartnerspress.org
Manufactured in the United States of America

Contents

Introduction

Year One. The first year of anything – a new job, a new place to live, a new relationship – brings with it a mixture of emotions, challenges, opportunities, and experiences that are unrivaled by any other time. When you are new at something, you see it with the freshest eyes you will ever have. It is the time of greatest excitement and anticipation, when everything may seem interesting and shiny and bright. It's also the time with the greatest potential for feelings of impostor syndrome, that feeling of questioning your own worth, your belonging, and your ability to be successful in this new place. Year One is the time to loosen your hold on what was known and familiar, to embrace something new and uncertain, which for some people is full of excitement and anticipation, and for others can contain moments of anxiety and dread.

Think back to your first year of college. You probably felt a little mixture of both: a little excited *and* a little anxious, unsure of that new place and how you fit into it. You may have adopted a "fake it til you make it" attitude, jumping in with both feet, joining everything you could, acting like it was the best thing that ever happened to you, which it might have been. You may have treaded those waters a little carefully, trying a few things out, latching onto any relationships you could find, feeling a bit homesick and off-balance. You may have had the freedom and the privilege of being a full-time student, or you may have had to balance your schoolwork with employment. You may have had some home and family obligations that seemed unlike those of your classmates. No matter what your experience was, you had to learn some things. You had to learn how to be a college student. You had to learn how to navigate a new place. You had to learn how to find your people. And that took time. But eventually you did it, and those experiences and that knowledge brought you to the place where you are now.

So, you've graduated from college, now fully an expert on that experience. And once again, you must wade through transition, learn a new place, find new people, figure out the rules for success. Except, unlike the high school to college transition, the college to work and life after college transition is a bit different. Sure, you may have had internships and summer jobs along the way, you may have worked throughout your college-going years, and those experiences *sort of* prepared you for this. But it's different when you're doing something for a finite amount of time, than when you're stepping into the rest of your life.

The experience of full-time work and adulthood are structurally unlike anything else you've done previously as a student. For example, nothing about work and life, unless you work in education, is organized by semesters. There are no more course syllabi, no more grades. The rules for success are different and will be different depending on your organization and your role. The things you are figuring out may be different than those of your peers working at other organizations or living in different locations or who have had different college experiences than you. You may be living on your own now, completely, for the first time, and that brings with it a set of new challenges and experiences, including paying your bills, building credit, feeding yourself, managing your wellbeing, building adult relationships, managing your time, finding hobbies, and so on. For some of you, this won't be completely new. But for others, this experience of being a working professional will require skills, knowledge, and resources that may feel a bit unfamiliar at first.

All of which makes it sound like a huge downer. But we promise, it's not! No matter your experience, there is something amazing happening right now that should be recognized and honored. You are, officially, an adult out in the world, no longer a student, unless you are choosing to continue your education in graduate school, which is what you've been working towards your whole life. This is the big payoff moment. This is the time when you get to use that great wisdom and knowledge you gained in college and make intentional decisions about who you are going to be moving forward, what you are going to do with your time and your experience, and with whom you will do it. This is your life, so embrace it, and dive into this moment and know that you absolutely are ready for what is to come.

As co-authors and colleagues, we spend a lot of time talking and thinking about these topics through our work with the Mentoring Resource Center and the Alumni Personal and Career Development Center, both part of the Office of Personal and Career Development at Wake Forest University. Much of the work of our Centers focuses on the first five years after college, a key period of transition and learning. We created our *Five For*

Your First Five™ model to do a deep dive into the five competencies that we believe every young professional should master in their first five years after college: Do the Work, Build a Life, Create Community, Practice Reflection, and Own What's Next.

Here, we focus specifically on Year One. This first year after college isn't the only year that matters, but it is a decisive moment that either can be lost to a fog of new experiences and emotions, or it can be an opportunity to embrace this new stage of your life with intention and compassion for yourself. In these pages, we want to provide you with the wisdom of our own experiences and point out potential challenges and opportunities to grow and to learn.

We create this text with recognition that everyone is in a different place. As we wrote these pages, we were fully immersed in COVID work-from-home realities, which necessarily impacted both our work and our lives. You too may be working remotely as you read this. You may be fully employed and living in a new city. You may still be seeking full-time employment and working a combination of part-time jobs to get by or living at home with your family again while you look for something more permanent. You may be starting graduate school. There are as many unique experiences as there are people, and there is no way that we can address all these experiences, here. Indeed, we recognize these pages are highly privileged towards the experience of the full-time working professional, which may not reflect your current reality. We invite you to take this perspective, use what works for you, and discard the rest while seeking out additional resources and guidance that will be helpful to you and your individual journey.

Our own experiences are unique as well, which is part of the reason we decided to write this together. Katherine spent her Year One in a post-graduate fellowship in our office here at Wake Forest. Her experience in that fellowship, and our ongoing conversations together about her experience, inspired the idea for this book, as much of her fellowship is an in-depth crash course on young professional development, both for her and for those of us who are mentoring and managing her. Allison has served as both manager and formal mentor to Katherine during this year, and is an experienced professional and manager in higher education, with a Ph.D. She has spent twenty-five-plus years working with professionals in all sectors and at all stages of career development, and draws upon that knowledge and that experience, here. But higher education is a specific industry and some of our experiences may not translate to individuals working in other fields or sectors.

It's also important to note that we are two white, American, Christian, cisgender, able-bodied women, who have both graduated from the same elite, predominately white institution (PWI). Those labels, histories, and experiences certainly shape who we are and how we experience the world, which may be different from you who are reading this. We will note, where it is appropriate, issues of diversity, equity, and inclusion that may be present or need to be highlighted; that said, this is not a book on workplace DEI nor would we want to present ourselves as experts on those topics. Instead, we point you to some resources we have found valuable as we explore our own experiences and privileges in this world, and hope you will find them useful as you continue to seek out additional ways of learning, knowing, and being.[1]

We have structured this book as part reflection, part instruction, part conversation between ourselves, as well as between us and you, the reader. It contains advice for both new graduates and for their managers, to answer one simple question: *how do you make the most of this year?* We start with that first point of transition, graduation, and then move through the first days and weeks of work, and the first weeks and months of life as a newly minted college educated professional. The chapters that follow aren't chronological, per se, but cover a range of topics we know will come up for you at some point over the next year.

Each chapter starts with a reflection by Katherine on her experience in Year One. Then we take a deep look at the topics together, bringing in research, tools, and strategies to advise first the new professional and then the manager. At the end of each section we provide questions to encourage both new professionals and managers to build deep reflection into your life as a core developmental practice. Throughout, we hope you will use these four questions as a guide:

- How am I building intentional relationships by being present with other people?
- What are six-month to one-year goals I can set for my ongoing growth and development?

- How am I seeking feedback on my strengths and growth areas?
- What am I learning? How can I use that knowledge in the future?

Our hope is that if you are a new professional, you will read this with your manager or someone you consider your mentor and discuss what you are experiencing and learning about yourself. Managers, we hope you will do the same: ask your new employee to work through this book with you for a deeper, more enriching professional relationship.

We are so grateful that you picked up this book, and we hope that it will be a helpful touchstone for you as you experience your Year One. It's an important year, quite possibly the most important one you will have. So, let's get started and make sure it's a great one.

1. So, I've Graduated. Now What?

Katherine's Experience

Who decided I was ready for this? I asked myself that question many, many times in the weeks following graduation. Who decided it was a good idea to give me consistent structure for the past four years, only to punt me into an adult life as soon as my diploma arrived in the mail? Who said it was fair for the friends I made over the past four years to scatter across the country over the course of a few weeks? Who said I was ready to be in control of my entire life: my location, my job, my money, my time, my community?

These questions swam around my mind after graduation. They might sound a little foolish, but to me they sounded like the most rational questions in the world. Are you asking yourself similar questions?

If so, I wonder if they are having the same effect on you as they did on me. They can cause you to be a hesitant decision-maker. They might make you say "no" instead of "yes" when someone asks you to go for coffee. They might give you intense writer's block at work because you're stuck in your own head. They might be the questions that keep you up at night as you wonder if you made the right decision over where to live.

I think these questions come from a voice in all of us, the one that chastises, underestimates, misremembers, and *lies*. The same one that told you that you wouldn't get into college or you'd never get a job. The one that says, "you're not ready, you're not capable, and you're not enough."

But, did you catch what I said there? That voice *lies*! The more I gain experience out here in the "real world," the more distanced I am from those first weeks full of sneaky questioning, the more aware I am of their absurdity and falsity and truths about my own abilities and strengths.

I recently got my diploma framed. Sometimes, I look up at it on my wall and see a regular old piece of paper. But other times, I see my diploma as a reminder that all my questions do not come from a place of truth. Your diploma is a piece of perfect paper that you can hold in your hands, the same hands that typed up all the essays, solved the equations, turned the pages of the textbooks and novels, swiped the paint across the canvas. You can run your fingers across the fancy lettering on that page and trace your name, first, middle, and last, and the degree that you earned. You earned that! And if that's not enough, look at the signatures around the university seal. There: approvals of important, trustworthy people who believe that you're ready. Those people, and many more they represent, prepared you over the past four years for what is to come.

Your friends, the ones who have scattered across the country? Those people are evidence that you are worth getting to know. Some of them you will keep, even if there is some distance between you now. And they are evidence that you'll make new friends again. In the meantime, having friends across the country means that you have a couch to sleep on no matter where you are and hope that you'll find your people again.

So, to answer those questions from earlier, *you* allowed yourself to be released into the adult world. You put hours and hours towards work and relationships for the past four years. You *are* ready to make your own decisions. You *are* ready to choose where you want to live, what you want to do, when you want to do it, who you want to do it alongside. You won't be an expert, but you are ready to begin. You didn't do it alone, and you don't have to do it alone now.

One of my favorite song lyrics says, "Kill the doubt that strangles my self-worth."[2] Isn't it the truth that doubt can so often take power over our identities? So, this is me telling you: Kill the doubt that strangles your self-worth. This is work, but it's essential. It's a slow and personal process, and I have full confidence that you'll figure it out on your own. The sooner you know your worth and kill your doubts, the sooner you'll claim your adulthood.

Advice for the New Professional

As Katherine's experience demonstrates, the move from college to work and life after college can be, at times, a rollercoaster of emotions. You may be excited, or nervous, or anxious, or a combination of all three. The idea of leaving the safety and security of what you have known for the past four years to go somewhere with a ton of unknowns may give you a feeling of dread and sadness. Or, you may be beyond ready to make that leap, to say goodbye to college and hello to that new, professional version of you. You know what? It's all OK. This is a big point of transition in your life. And it's one of the last shared experiences you will have marking a move to something new. It's important to acknowledge it and to honor where you are, right now.

You made the move from high school to college along with your peers, and you figured that out. Now you're making the move from college to life after college alongside your college classmates, and you each must figure that out in your own ways. But after this there won't necessarily be these big marquee moments that you do alongside a group going through the same thing at the same time. You might get married, you might buy a house, you might have kids, you might get a big promotion, you might move across the country or across the world. You might do all these things, or you might not. You will do or not do each of those things on your own time and to fit your own needs and interests as determined by you.

Here's the thing about transition: it's a deeply personal experience. We like to refer to a model, created by the organizational development expert William Bridges, to explain exactly what happens during these times.[3] First, it's important to recognize the difference between the terms "change" and "transition." Change is about external events or situations. It's a thing that happens to you, like finishing college. Change is something you can point to or name.

Transition, on the other hand, "is the inner psychological process that people go through as they internalize and come to terms with the new situation that the change brings about."[4] It can be easy to focus on the change alone, as something to be managed or dealt with, or a desired outcome to achieve. Ignore the transition process at your peril. There is something important that happens inside you during times of change, emotionally, mentally, even sometimes physically, that must be honored. And it happens for each of us individually. In other words, your process of transition may not look like or feel like anyone else's, even though you are experiencing the same change event.

Second, there are three critical stages to the transition process, according to Bridges. It starts with an ending. This is when you are asked to let go of something familiar, possibly something that feels safe and comfortable. Even if you are ready to let go and leave it behind you, there are a lot of knowns there. You know the rules for behavior, you know the expectations, you know the people. For you, right now, the ending you are letting go of is your college experience. It may also be your college identity, the person you were known as, or the person you see yourself as when you look in the mirror.

Next you pass through the neutral zone. This is when you're in a bit of free-fall, no longer tied to the past but not yet attached to what is to come. You haven't fully committed. For some, this feels like freedom. There aren't as many rules or expectations. For others, this feels incredibly uncomfortable. You may be in this stage currently, in between graduation and moving to a new city or starting that new job. You may even stay here for a bit after you have made that move and before you fully commit to that new life and role.

And then, finally, you reach a new beginning. You have to learn new rules, new expectations, new people. You have to take on your new identity as a working professional adult, fully capable of taking care of yourself and your needs, as well as managing your career and next steps. You, like Katherine, may be asking, *Who decided I was ready for this?*

We each go through these three stages of transition at different paces and with different emotions. You might race through that neutral zone, eager to get to the new beginning, while someone else is clinging onto that ending by the very ends of their fingers, terrified about what's to come. You might be fully ready to leave college behind, to create your new adult professional self out in the world. One of your friends might be sad to let go of that college existence, while another might want to hang out in that neutral zone for a while. No matter where you are in the process, we all have to go through each of the three stages. So, it's important to recognize where you are, why you're there, and how you feel about it. Transition isn't easy because transition is personal and it's emotional.

But the good news is, while your new beginning may look and feel different from what you're leaving behind, there is a lot about what's happened up to this point that has been getting you ready for this moment. Because, while there are a lot of differences between college and life and work after college, there are some similarities, too. You can draw upon those similarities and everything you have learned about yourself over the past four years to be successful here.

Let's start with some key differences. You might think of this as the point when the training wheels come off. No longer are there tons of people and resources and offices set up, just for you, to make sure that you are successful here. You have to seek those things out on your own. You may have spent the past four years living in a residence hall, going to student health, using the university counseling center and career office, eating off a meal plan, and, generally speaking, living off the bank of mom and dad or student loans. And now you are on your own, figuring out how to feed and take care of yourself, and possibly responsible for your own finances for the first time. Those student loans may be starting to come due. While you may have felt pretty restricted by college life and ready for this next phase, there was a comfort in the familiarity that was college. Or, for some of you, this may feel like a relief, as you no longer have to balance work and classes and the expectations of your college experience. You no longer have to try to fit into a place that may not look like you or feel like it fully supports who you are.

On the other hand, it's not *that* different. Yes, the structure changes when you graduate. The way you spend your time changes. The ways you spend your days change. But the hidden secret to the educational process is that it has been structured to give you those training wheels in order to slowly, over time, give you a little more freedom, a little more control over your choices and decisions, to prepare you for this moment. You have had to figure out how to be successful in a new place before. You have had to figure out how to manage your time and competing priorities before. Sure, it's not all handed to you now, but you do have all the tools and skills inside you to be successful here. Remember that. You're ready. For those of you who have been balancing work and school these past four years, you have gained tremendous skills for managing your time and your priorities that will serve you well, now. And, if you felt like you didn't fully fit into that place, the good news is this: you have gained deep awareness about who you are and what you need to be successful. Now you get to put that wisdom to work for you.

- What are those inner voices of self-doubt saying to you right now? Why do you think you are hearing those messages of self-doubt?
- Where do you see yourself in the transition process: ending, neutral zone, or new beginning? How do you feel about this position?
- When you look back on college, what are two or three strategies that helped you to be successful there? How can you use those strategies to be successful where you are now?

Advice for Managers

For those of you in the role of manager to a new graduate, it's worth noting that this young person was a senior in college just a few months or even just a few weeks ago. Nothing magic has happened during this time. They didn't suddenly figure out how to be a professional, or gain a bunch of skills, or acquire ten years of experience or a master's degree. And, as noted in the previous pages, a lot of change is happening for them. Even if they're showing up every day with their game face on, seemingly ready to work and to contribute, there's a lot that's happening for them emotionally. A little compassion, empathy, and connection will go a long way towards you helping them to be as successful as possible.

Not everyone goes through this period of transition in the same ways. Your new professional may be fully ready to embrace their adult self out in the world, or they may be in an in-between phase, no longer a college student but not yet sure who they are, personally or professionally. They may have spent the past few years working while going to school and upholding many other commitments and feel quite confident about who they are in this moment. Or, as Katherine notes, they might be experiencing a good amount of self-doubt about their skills, abilities, and competence in the workplace and in life. They are likely experiencing a lot of new things – new job, new home, new city, new financial freedom or responsibilities, new relationships, and more – all at once. When was the last time you changed absolutely everything about your life all at the same time? You can imagine how overwhelming that might feel.

During this time of transition, your job as a manager is to show them the ropes. In the next chapter we will talk about the importance of this intentional onboarding process and how to do this. In a later chapter we will discuss the importance of scaffolding skills through intentional learning experiences. This is the bottom line: don't expect new employees to be doing college level work when they are in fact still in grade school, professionally-speaking. It is absolutely worth the time and the effort to get to know them as people, to figure out what their strengths and interests are, and to give them the tools and the information that they need to perform their roles to your expectations. By setting them up for success now, you increase the likelihood that they will continue to meet your expectations later.

Part of this work is teaching them the *why* behind the work of your organization. Spend some time in intentional conversation about the people you serve and how this work makes an impact and show how the work that this new professional will be doing is going to make an impact as well. These things aren't always as obvious as they seem, but they have tremendous effects on employee engagement and morale. Because the truth is, this new employee may not be as excited about the work as you are. They may have taken this role because it aligns with their passion and their internal calling. Or, maybe they took it because it seemed like a good next step. They might have taken it because it pays the bills or allowed them to move to a city where they wanted to live. Not everyone needs to be following a calling. But understanding the *why* behind the work will help them connect their daily tasks to something that is bigger than they are.

Spend some time early on talking about this transition stage they are currently experiencing. As we noted in the previous section, there are three distinction stages to every transition: endings, the neutral zone, and a new beginning. Talk about where they are and how that might be impacting their ability to be fully present now. Ask thoughtful questions about the challenges they are facing and provide recommendations about how they can approach these challenges. No matter one's experience level, when we move to a new place or take on a new role we all can use a little help figuring out where we are and how to be successful there. Your new employee is no different. So, put extra effort into being that supportive ear, that voice of reassurance, and that wise counselor right now. After all, this isn't just your new employee. This is a human being with emotions and struggles and doubts just like everyone else. Demonstrating a bit of genuine care will go a long way towards their success in this Year One.

Questions for Reflection

- What are some challenges your new employee might be struggling with right now? How can you support them with those challenges?
- What is the *why* behind your organization's work? How are you communicating that?
- Where is your new employee in the three stages of transition? What would help them to fully embrace this position and thrive in this new beginning?

2. First Days, First Weeks – Figuring Out Work

Katherine's Experience

During my first few weeks of work I remember feeling a lot of mixed emotions.

Some days, I woke up giddy to start the day and learn something new. Even though I began my job virtually, I was excited to put on my new work clothes and accomplish something. I enjoyed the rhythm of the workday. I liked that my work ended basically at 5 o'clock each day so I could spend time with my roommates, cook, and relax. I appreciated going to work (even if that meant checking in remotely) and feeling respected, like a true adult and not like a "kid." I felt proud that I had a degree and experiences that made me capable of handling a task all on my own.

Of course, you may not be surprised to hear that there were many days that did *not* feel like this. Pretty soon, the luster wore off my "home office" and I began to see it for what it really was: a hand-me-down desk sitting in my bedroom. As my workload built up, I struggled to manage my time and prioritize important tasks.

I realized that the respect I received (and for which I am thankful) brings with it a great responsibility. It sunk in that a mistake on my part could affect a whole team of people, unlike my student years, when my decisions mostly only affected me.

I was shocked at how tired I felt at the close of each workday (and, if I'm being honest, in the middle of many workdays too). I sat in one place all day long and yet I was mentally and even physically taxed at the end of each day.

But, slowly, I started to adapt.

I remembered that "an object in motion stays in motion," which meant that getting up from my desk to move during the day, along with a quick, brief walk at the end of my work day, kept me energized and feeling less sluggish.

I found tools to stay motivated throughout my workday, like talking to a roommate for a few minutes during a break, or having an encouraging morning routine, or listening to a relaxing podcast during lunch. I began to figure out how to manage my time. I learned how to make my room (slash: office) a place where I was excited to spend most of my time. I started to figure out how to show up and do work, how to meet my new coworkers' expectations, and how to ask for guidance and direction when I needed it. And I learned to give myself some grace when I didn't get it all right at first.

As in any season of life, I reminded myself that joy and struggle are almost always mixed. I began to appreciate the wonderful things about this time in my life, and I began to accept the difficult aspects I will never be able to change. Eventually, I found that there is a whole lot to be said for giving yourself a break when you need it, asking for help when you need it, and a change in perspective!

Advice for the New Professional

The first days and weeks of work after graduating, while unique to your personal situation, will be unlike most experiences you've had previously. Sure, you may have had internships and summer jobs, you may have worked throughout college either on-campus or off. But many of those are short-time experiences, with a clear end date and often contain limited opportunity for growth as a result.

This is not like that. First, there is no end date here, unless, like Katherine, you have joined a specific, time-limited opportunity. Second, while you might be excited about these first days and weeks of work, there is a strong chance that many other people won't be, or at least not to the same degree you are. Why? Because they have their own stuff to worry about, that has nothing to do with you. While a few of you may have been hired as the CEO of something, for most of you, you're just the new low-level staff person, expected to show up and do what is expected of you. Every day. And one of the most important tasks for you to do right now is to figure out what those expectations are.

Hopefully, there will be a structured and organized onboarding process, complete with clearly articulated rules and norms of behavior, facilitated introductions and connections to people throughout the organization, instructions on how to show up and do work to meet your manager's expectations, and even formal processes of mentoring and coaching provided to support your transition into and your ongoing growth and development within the organization. Hopefully, you will be surrounded by people who truly want to help you succeed.

Unfortunately, not every organization is great at onboarding and supporting that new employee transition process, so there's a chance that you will not be surrounded by people cheering your success. It's not because your new colleagues are terrible people, they've got their own things to worry about and you can't always be their priority. It's ultimately your responsibility to figure out work. In fact, one of the keys to being a rock-star young professional is to recognize that it's on you to take ownership of your career and your growth, to seek out opportunities, to learn what you need to know to be successful, and to build the relationships that are going to help you get there. In other words, don't just wait for someone to hand these things to you, and then wonder why they don't.

The first days and weeks of any new position – both now and in the future (because this won't be the last time that you're the "new person") – have the potential to be overwhelming and jarring and as Katherine notes, pretty tiring. They can be a blur of new people, and if you're going into an office, new spaces, to learn about. You might be handed a list of new responsibilities and instructions on how to accomplish them. Or, you might not be given any information at all and you're left wondering how you're supposed to fill your time. The whole team might welcome you with a social gathering, or not. You might be made to feel like a valued member of the organization, or not.

Long-term, these are all things to pay attention to, because they speak to the culture of the organization. For right now, it's important to note, you don't control any of this. What you can control is how *you* show up, how *you* engage with people, and how *you* seek out knowledge and opportunity and manage your energy and productivity. And remember that whether they do this onboarding process well or not, people will be paying attention to how you behave in this moment.

Your first day or days should include some kind of human resources orientation, where you will learn about policies and procedures, hopefully get the opportunity to sign up for health coverage and retirement funds if those things are provided, and learn about other valuable parts of your new working life. While thinking about things like parking passes and tax documents and non-discrimination policies and so forth may leave you less than energized, it's important to remember: this is your money, your health, your role, your organization, and your commitment to uphold certain laws and policies. Arguably, these are some of the most important meetings you ever will have, at work. So, pay attention, ask questions, and take these conversations seriously. Be sure to seek out guidance from trained professionals or wise counselors when you need it. And if you are in a workplace without an HR department, like many early-stage start-ups, be sure to look for external resources and guidance to help you in this moment.

The first days and weeks of any new role are a fantastic learning opportunity. Never again will you have this much of an outsider's view, untarnished by the perspectives and opinions that you will start to form in the coming months. This is an ideal time to ask questions, to take notes on your impressions, to meet as many people as you can across the organization. Embrace being "the new person." The new person gets to ask all the seemingly stupid questions (which aren't remotely stupid) that everyone else is dying to ask, but they don't because they think they should know better. The new person gets to spend time with people, learning about their roles and responsibilities, with zero angle other than just wanting to learn. The new person often has the best view into the power structures and the organizational culture, because it's completely unfiltered. Take some notes, ask thoughtful questions, and reflect on what you are learning. At a minimum, this is a great way to start to build relationships with your new colleagues.

And, remember, you will be in this position again. Many times, in fact. At some point you will leave this organization for another, or you will take on a new role with a new team, or even just take on new responsibilities where you are. You will be the new person, once again. So, take note of what's working for you, now, and what's not, and the things you are learning, so the next time you are the new person it won't feel so *new*.

As you get started, here are a few key strategies you can use to take advantage of these first days and weeks:

- **Get clear on the rules and norms for behavior.** Ask questions of your manager and colleagues, and then pay attention to what people actually do. If you are told that everyone works from 8-5, but start noticing that when you arrive at 8 am, everyone is already at their desks and working, then you better start showing up earlier. Generally, norms of behavior show up in actual practice more so than in stated expectations.
- **Set some goals.** Hopefully your manager will work with you to create a set of goals for your work. If they don't, it doesn't mean you can't set them for yourself. Think about what you want to learn in your first month, in your first three months, and your first six months. Then, take these goals to your manager for some additional feedback. Not only will this demonstrate that you are taking ownership for your growth, it will also help to clarify expectations for your work. (We'll talk more specifically about goal setting in chapter five.)
- **Seek out conversations.** Set up short coffee conversations with people to get to know them, their role and responsibilities, the projects they are working on, and to seek out advice. Not only will this start to develop great relationships which will pay off down the road, it can also lead to work! You may find a project that you can join, or an opportunity to help a colleague. Be sure to let your manager know that you are having these conversations so they know how you are spending your time.
- **Ask for regular meetings with your manager.** Hopefully, your manager will set up regular check-in meetings with you to discuss your work and your progress. But if they don't, it doesn't mean you can't ask for it. Come to these meetings with an agenda to make the most of their time. Ask pointed questions about your goals, your work assignments, and what you need to know and do to be successful there. Over time, you should need these sorts of feedback conversations less frequently as you become comfortable in your role and the organization.

The first days and weeks in any new position are a learning opportunity like no other. This is your opportunity to begin to explore the type of professional you want to be. Every day that you show up to work, every interaction that you have, communicates to others who you are, just as they are doing so, to you. Pay attention and be intentional. It all matters.

Questions for Reflection

- What are your first impressions of your role, team, and organization?
- What do you not know, and what questions can you ask to start to learn about your role, team, and organization?
- Who are three or four people you can reach out to this week to set up a coffee conversation?

Advice for Managers

With the best of intentions, organizations sometimes bring on new people and forget to plan for their arrival. This happens with people at all levels of experience. Older, more seasoned employees are better able to navigate through these uncertain waters. (It still doesn't make it a great strategy.) But for brand-new employees this lack of structured onboarding can have devastating impacts. Remember, they don't know what they don't know. They shouldn't know how to show up and be successful in these roles or within your organization. Everything that happens during this time is teaching them how to behave and expectations for what a successful professional looks and acts like, not to mention delivering clear messages about whether they belong there. So, be intentional. Be thoughtful. And think about what you would want if you were in their shoes.

The first few days and weeks of any new position are a critical learning opportunity both for the new employee and for you. Take the time to put together a strategic onboarding plan. This should include expectations for work and behavior, the key people they should meet during the first few weeks and a plan for those conversations, and a detailed outline of how they will spend their very first days and weeks. There is nothing worse for a new employee than to show up on day one and be told, "We'll give you some time to get settled." Do you know how long that process takes? About five minutes. Then what are they supposed to do?

As the manager, set some regular check-in meetings. Ideally, for the first week, these should be daily, and then taper off from there. Set and communicate clear expectations for the work and for professionalism. One of the worst things you can do is to make assumptions that this person knows what to do and how to do it well. Why should they? They've never worked for you before. There is no reason to make their professional success a mystery they need to solve. There is zero value to the professional hazing that frequently occurs within organizations.

Help your new employee set goals and identify some short-term work projects. Have a project ready for them to work on during their first few weeks. This will give them something productive to do with their time and help them to learn how to do work well for you. It will also give you an opportunity to have explicit conversations about the work, their process, and your expectations. Remember that every one of these conversations is a teaching and coaching opportunity for you, demonstrating through concrete actions what it looks like to set professional goals, to be a competent professional, and to show up with you and with others. These sorts of "life lessons" are as important as the work itself, and not to be missed.

Just as this is a key learning moment for the employee, it's also a great opportunity for you to learn from them. As noted in the prior section, your new employees are some of the best sources of knowledge and feedback on what is happening within your organization, because they see it with fresh eyes not yet clouded by internal experiences, perspectives, or cynicism. Be intentional about asking questions of them as they are doing work and having introductory conversations with their new colleagues. This is a great chance for you to learn something about your organization that you might be missing. Make it a safe conversation. Your employees don't need to be put into the position of reporting back to you. But if you are open to the feedback and the learning, you can discover some great opportunities for personal and organizational growth.

Finally, let's not forget that your new employee is experiencing a whole new set of emotions during this time. They're in a new place, with new people, many of whom likely aren't in their peer group. This role might be their dream job, or it might be the job they were able to get. They may not share your enthusiasm and excitement for the work that you are doing, and that's OK. They may not see how this role fits into their long-term career plans. As Katherine reflects, at some point in these first few weeks they're going to become exceptionally tired, because they're not yet used to showing up day after day and doing work. They don't yet know how to regulate their emotions and reactions to what happens in the workplace.

All of which is to say, these are great topics for conversation. Be an intentional and supportive manager. Your employee should not be expected to share everything with you, but you can certainly talk about the challenges of work just as much as you talk about the tasks and deadlines. Talk about how your role fits into your long-term career plan, and how you have figured that out. Talk about strategies you have learned to manage work-life balance and for managing your time effectively.

If you don't feel comfortable having these conversations, or if your employee doesn't feel comfortable with it, offer to connect them with someone who can serve as a confidential mentor and sounding board. Not every employee will want it. Not everyone wants to share everything about their lives at work. And that's OK. Especially if your employee does not fit into those white, cisgender, able-bodied norms that many organizations tend to privilege, they may not feel comfortable sharing their whole lives with you, or anyone else. There may be real risk there for them to do so, both personally and professionally. As a manager, your job is not to force them into these conversations, but to think about how you are creating an organization that supports and uplifts all your employees. You need to remember that your employees are whole people, with lives and families and backgrounds and challenges that come with them to work, every day. To pretend otherwise does them, the organization, and the work a great disservice.

Questions for Reflection

- How are you creating a thoughtful and intentional onboarding process for your new employee? What needs to happen in their first days and weeks so that they feel like they belong?
- What does your employee need to know to be successful in their role? What are your expectations for their work?
- What can you share about your own challenges and strategies for managing work, finding balance, and managing time that might be helpful to your new employee?

3. First Weeks, First Months – Figuring Out Life

Katherine's Experience

Before graduating, I had this vision for post-grad life: every morning would be slow, with plenty of time to exercise before work. Then, I'd get my work done an hour early – because I am so efficient working from home – and have an hour to go for a walk before meeting my friends for happy hour. For dinner, I'd make a healthy and colorful meal like a pomegranate chicken with vegetables on the side, that would pair perfectly with my fancy sparkling water in my brand-new glassware. I'd host a friend for dinner every evening. After I washed my shiny new plates and silverware, there would be plenty of time left for myself to relax, get ready for bed, watch a show, *and* read. I would get to bed in plenty of time to be well-rested the next day.

Sounds attainable, right? You're probably shaking your head right now, but I really thought so. I forgot about the time it takes to shower and get ready for work after exercising in the morning. I forgot that you can't just rush through your work; there's too much of it not to take breaks, not to mention wanting to do it well. Pomegranates are expensive, and drinks are expensive, and I've discovered that I am never going to buy name-brand sparkling water when I can buy the off-brand. I didn't take into account travel time to and from work when I go into the office, the cost of gas, and the fact that I have to pay the security deposit for my apartment and the start-up fees for my utilities. So, I'll be taking my cousin's hand-me-down plates, silverware, and juice glasses, thank you very much. And, let's swap out dinner with a friend for Facetime while I'm eating, cancel those drinks, and reserve a few minutes every day for an existential crisis.

Wow. Please hear me out. I don't tell you this to disappoint you. But here's the thing: this narrative – the realistic one – this applies to *everyone* in their twenties. Even those people who post their perfect dinners, perfect walks, and perfect friends on their Instagram story. When you pull back the curtain on Year One, you'll find that everyone is just doing their best. No one has balance yet, or very many friends, or a whole lot of energy.

Learning to manage my expectations of my first year post-graduation with reality and actively not comparing myself to others were two of the best things I did right from the start. Here is why you are allowed to lower your expectations a little bit: it will get better. You can lower your expectations with hope and anticipation of what is to come in the future, where you will learn how to balance your life and your bank account, learn how to cook, and figure out strategies to manage your workload and energy. Just remember, it will take time, and it will happen at your own pace, just as it is supposed to do. Set small goals in the beginning and then you can slowly raise them over time. I am so glad I gave myself the grace to do that in this first year after college.

It meant that during my very first weeks living on my own I knew that I wasn't going to be making fancy meals, or even very healthy ones. But that's okay because my goal for that first week was just to stay alive, fill my belly at each meal, and not overshoot what I needed and end up throwing a lot of food away. So, I spent $12 on pasta, pasta sauce, turkey, cheese, bread, cereal, milk, olive oil, and eggs. Was I tired of eating gluten by the end of that first week? You bet. But was I doing the best I could and feeding my body? You bet!

The next week, after I had unpacked most of my boxes and set up a desk to work from home, I was able to add two or three vegetables and fruits to my grocery trip. The next week, I got a few vegetables from the farmer's market and realized that their petite sizes worked a lot better for feeding just one person. The week after that, I bought meat at the grocery store to cook and learned how to freeze food when I made too big a portion.

When it came to my home, it was important for me not to expect for my space to feel finished the day, or even the week, after moving in. It was enough to just have a place to sleep, a place to cook, and a place to eat. It was okay that I waited until my second month to invest in a bookshelf or until my third month to finally get things hung up on the walls. Pace yourself as you spend time and money making your space feel like home.

Let your sleep schedule grow as you figure out what works for you. Give yourself time to build new relationships and to figure out how to maintain the old ones, and to learn where you're living. If you are in a new place you won't immediately know all the best walking spots, the best grocery store, the best social groups to join. So, take it slow. Over time you'll find your place and your people and the rhythm that works for you.

Advice for the New Professional

Just like the start of your first post-college job may be different from previous work experiences you have had, creating a life that aligns with who you are becoming after college can be different than prior experiences you have had. This transition is no less important. After all, work is just one part of who you are as an actual living, breathing, functioning person out in the world. Your work – what you have chosen to do and where you have chosen to do it – will impact your life in many ways. The people you go to work with will leave impacts as well, which we will discuss in the next chapter. This is the start of the rest of your life, and it's a moment that needs to be acknowledged and celebrated. As with everything that is to come, you have a choice: you can let life happen to you, or you can walk into it with intention. You can probably imagine what we are hoping you will do.

You may have had the experience of living on your own before, maybe during college or during one or more of your summers. You may have had the experience of shopping for groceries and fixing your own meals, paying your bills, and managing your time. Those are great experiences to draw upon now. Think about what worked for you and how you can apply those lessons to better navigate this experience of showing up to your life every day.

And, this is your opportunity to create an intentional life for yourself, an adult life that honors who you are and what's important to you. It's time to get focused on how you are going to manage some key resources that belong solely to you: your time, your energy, and your money. Let's start with your time and energy.

As Katherine has mentioned, the pace of life as a working professional is different from that of a student, and in the first few weeks you may be incredibly tired. It's going to hit you like a tidal wave. First you may be pumped up and motivated about this new experience and running on adrenaline and nervous energy. Much like you did in college, you may try to fill every bit of downtime you have with something "productive." You may say yes to social engagements and join a gym and sign up to volunteer and make sure every hour of every day has something in it from the time you get up until the time your head hits the pillow at night. Or, you may feel a sense of anxiety because you aren't able to fill those hours with things you normally would, and yet you feel like you should be doing *something*.

And then what happens? The adrenaline is going to wear off. Work will get busy. You are going to experience a level of tiredness that you haven't before, and you will realize that being at work, even if work is sitting at a desk all day (sometimes, especially then) can be exhausting. And it's even more exhausting if you are running on fumes. The bottom line is that burning the candle at both ends isn't going to take you very far in the working world. How you show up every day says something about you to your colleagues. Yawning through a meeting or losing focus on a project because you can't keep your eyes open isn't exactly the best impression for you to make. Plus, you don't want to feel tired all the time, either.

On top of which, you have a lot of things you need to get done that will fill your available time. As Katherine described, you have to find a grocery that will fit into your budget. You have to fix meals. You have to do laundry and clean your house. You have to stay in touch with friends and family and take care of your health by getting some exercise. If you're going into an office, there is the commute to factor in. And if you work a regular 8-5 job (let's be honest, most jobs these days extend well beyond those hours), that only leaves you with a limited amount of time at the end of the day and on weekends to get these things done. Something has to give. And it's up to you to decide what that thing or things will be.

Our advice to you is to get comfortable with being uncomfortable, especially in these first few weeks and months. It's OK to have some alone time. You may still be setting things up, getting pictures on the walls, figuring out where the coffee pot should go, and so on. These might seem like small, silly activities, but it actually is important work! You will spend the majority of your time as an adult in one of two places: at work and in your home. No matter how much you love your job, work is never going to be completely fulfilling, every moment of the day. You will have bad days at work. We all do. So, take the time to make your home into a place you actually want to be, a place that feels supportive and comfortable.

Give yourself a few weeks, if not a few months, to figure out your patterns. What time does the workday actually end? When is it best for you to go to the gym or do some kind of exercise? For example, Allison has learned that, while she wouldn't call herself a morning person, if she's going to exercise it has to be first thing in the morning. And that affects what time she goes to bed and how she manages her time throughout the day. You might also get into a pattern of going to the grocery on the same day each week, starting to meal plan, even identifying a day of the week to do laundry. Figure out a pattern that works for you.

We recommend doing a time audit for yourself once you find a bit of a routine. Just take note of how you spend every hour of the day for a couple of weeks, and then assess how it looks. Just like with your finances, you may find that there are places you can make a cut, or additions you can make. The hard truth is we each only have twenty-four hours every day. If eight to ten of those are spent on work, two on meals, and you want to get at least eight hours of sleep, you've only got four to six hours with which to work. That may sound like a lot but throw in commuting (if you have one), working out, catching up with friends, doing some laundry, and you'll soon see how quickly it goes.

Before you start to fill every possible moment of that free time with something, give yourself some time to figure out what you're missing. For example, did you do a lot of service work in college? Is that a gap you would like to fill? Did you belong to a faith-based organization? Did you spend a lot of time playing intramural sports? While there isn't going to be an activities fair set up for you, these opportunities do exist in the real world, too. You just have to seek them out. The key is not to go looking for them all at once. Pick one. Just one. Make a commitment to it and see how it fits into your life. A few months from now you will have a much clearer sense of your time, your energy, and your desire to do these things than you do right now.

Next, let's talk about finances. This means not just focusing on long-term planning like retirement (which is important) but also getting smart about your short-term budgeting and spending. Just like with your time, start to track all the places you are spending money. Some of these will be one-time expenses that go along with setting up a home and moving to a new place. But soon you will start to notice a pattern with your "regular" expenses that is worth observing. Do you skip the coffee pot and hit up the coffee shop every morning for a $5 latte? That's $35 (or more) you're spending on coffee each week. That may not seem like much, but it adds up to over $1,800 a year. On coffee. Surely you have some other things you could do with $1,800. Do you pick the fancy grocery over the cheaper option? Are you shopping for clothes and other fun items on your credit card?

Listen. Your financial choices are your own. If you want that latte or that new outfit and you can afford it, go for it. The key is the phrase "and you can afford it." Far too many young people get into debt way too quickly and it's a hard place to escape. Staying on top of your finances, making a budget and sticking to it, being smart about saving (so that eventually you can start investing and *really* saving) are all hallmarks of being a smart, responsible adult. It doesn't matter how much disposable income you have, or if mom and dad are still footing the bill. There is no excuse for not knowing what your income versus your expenses are each month. The rise of things like Venmo and other apps can make this particularly challenging, so be hyper-aware of how much money you have going out versus coming in each month.

Just like tracking your time, creating and using a budget does not have to be difficult. You have a fixed amount of money coming in each month, and an identifiable set of expenses. Take a spreadsheet and name all of the categories you can think of where you spend money. These will include things like rent, utilities, groceries, eating out, and so on. Then, for several months, track every single dollar that you spend and take note of your patterns. Is there some place you can make a cut? Is there some place that needs additional resources? Once you have that, then you can create a budget, which is the target amounts or limits for each of those categories. By having those targets, you can start to make smart choices with your spending. For example, if you have budgeted a hundred dollars for dining out, and you have already met that limit, when someone asks you to meet them for dinner you have a choice to make: say yes, and take money from another category, or say no until the next month. You may find as you are just starting out that you basically are breaking even each month.

Eventually, you will find opportunities to put money into savings for your future. Getting into the habit of budgeting and smart financial choices, now, will allow you to make other choices, later.[5]

Finally, these first few months are also about finding your place. Find that coffee shop you love (for the occasional splurge!) and pick out your favorite grocery store. Take some time to wander this place, to find new neighborhoods, stores, or parts of town. Whether you moved to a big city or a small town, there exists a whole universe of people who are going about the business of living and working and building community there. Think about:

- What spaces do you occupy, what spaces do you want to occupy, and how can you do this?
- What are the supporting resources you need – think counselors, doctors, or other helping professionals – and how will you find them?
- In what ways can and will you contribute productively to your community?

You need to figure out how and where you fit in. Get comfortable with being uncomfortable for a while. Eventually you will find those places that uniquely suit who you are, your needs, your interests, and your values as you begin to build a life that works for you.

Questions for Reflection

- What has been your biggest challenge with building a life post-college? What is one strategy that could help you with that challenge?
- What are you learning about yourself from auditing your time and your energy? Where can you make positive changes?
- What steps can you take to begin to manage your finances effectively?

Historically, there was an unwritten rule that the boundaries between work and life should be clear and impermeable: you leave your life stuff at home and don't bring it to work (though not, for some reason, vice versa). As anyone who has worked for more than a minute knows, that's just not possible, and fortunately is no longer the case in most organizations. We are each complete humans with experiences and histories and worries and challenges and all sorts of other things happening outside of work that do in fact show up at work, no matter how hard we try to leave them behind. These things impact the work that we do, the ways in which we show up for one another, and even, for you, the ways in which you manage your employees. At a certain point, everyone has worked for the so-called "moody boss" whose interactions with their staff fluctuate based on how they are feeling. It's not the way that anyone deserves to be managed. But managers are imperfect humans, too.

The folks at Gallup have researched the levels of employee engagement across the world, and identified three types of employees: engaged, not engaged, or actively disengaged. In their most recent survey, from 2019, the percentage of engaged employees had risen to its highest level since the survey started in 2000, to 35 percent.[6] Of course, that means that roughly two-thirds of employees are either not engaged or actively disengaged. Why does this matter? Because teams with higher levels of engagement produce better outcomes, are less likely to leave the organization, are healthier, and experience less burnout.

Further, Gallup has identified the factors that help promote higher levels of engagement. They include caring about your people as individuals, connecting the work to meaning and purpose (the individual's, not yours), providing clear expectations for the work, and providing growth and development opportunities. These are the things that great managers do. And it starts with getting to know your people on an individual level, caring about who they are, why they come to work every day, and what they bring with them and what they may be leaving behind.

It's OK to talk to your people about their lives, as long as they are open to having that conversation with you. You don't need to be involved in their lives. But your people, and especially this new young professional, are in the middle of a full life, and much of it has nothing to do with work. You, as the manager, have an obligation to check in on your people and to help them to navigate these waters, which may seem on the face of it to have nothing to do with work. But at a minimum, it's certainly impacting how your people show up to work and may even impact their abilities to get the work done.

One way that you can be helpful is to ask how they are building a life outside of work and what challenges they are encountering. Offer advice based on your own experience. Think about:

- What have you learned about creating relationships as an adult?
- What has worked for you in terms of managing time and priorities?
- What do you know about the community and places or opportunities to get involved?

These are all fair game questions and conversation topics. It is one way you can get to know your employee as an individual, find out what they are interested in, and seek out ways to help. But to be clear, again, not all your employees will welcome these sorts of conversations and it should never be forced. They are there to do a job, not to share their personal lives with you. What may feel to you like a friendly conversation and one you initiate with the best of intentions can have harmful impacts. Whether you think there is or not, there is always a power differential between you and those you supervise. It is your job to recognize when you are stepping outside the boundaries of a manager-employee relationship in ways that make your employee uncomfortable.

It's possible you won't know all the answers. Allison likes to think of herself as a "with-it young professional" but the truth is she actually is a pretty tired mid-career professional. She shouldn't be anyone's go-to person for advice on how to make friends as a young adult. But she knows people in that stage of life, and she can be a great connector between Katherine and those people. She can suggest groups to join or places to look for more information. Sometimes the best thing that a person can do is to make a connection, to make an introduction, and then to get out of the way. You don't have to be their friend matchmaker, but we know that social isolation has devastating physical, emotional, and mental health impacts.[7] And those impacts will ultimately affect your employee's professional contributions. Help them get connected, or at least point them in the right direction.

Boundaries are important. You are not this person's counselor or their therapist. Nor are you their financial advisor or their parent. There is a difference between wanting to be a supportive, caring manager and wanting to be someone's friend and confidante. Your employee needs friends, needs people to vent to, needs people with whom to share office gossip. The effective manager knows when and how to set and maintain boundaries. Clear boundaries set the stage for clear expectations and effective relationships. Ultimately, your role is to manage this person's work. And that means getting clear on what is allowed within the work environment and what is not. You do not do your employee any favors by letting them slide on their work commitments simply because adulting is hard. Be clear about your expectations and hold them accountable. And, be compassionate about their struggles as a human.

Finally, it's worth noting that your new professional may show up to work with different expectations than you for what work-life balance looks like. They may fully expect to work out or run some personal errands in the middle of the day because they plan to work in the evening and they're always on and available on their phones and social media. Up to this point, their lives have not been scheduled in long blocks of time in one place. They are used to an hour here, an hour there, and more or less managing their own time as they see fit. Work is different. And your job is to help them to understand not only how it's different, but why.

Again, this is where clear expectations upfront make a tremendous difference. When do you expect people to be available and "on?" There is no clear-cut answer here because every organization is different. We hope in the future there is greater understanding for the need for flexibility for all employees no matter their stage of life. People should be able to go for a run in the middle of the day or see the doctor or run some errands. Some of your employees (mostly women) spent more than a year during the pandemic trying to maintain their workload, homeschool children, and take care of household obligations, with devastating impacts.[8] These difficulties certainly were enhanced during COVID times, but they weren't absent before just because they mostly went unseen or unrecognized. The 8-5 workday shackled to a desk is a holdover from another era that mostly no longer applies.

However, some jobs require a set schedule. If you are a teacher, you're expected to be in the classroom. If you're a doctor, you're expected to be with patients. You might have expectations that your employees be in the office at certain times. Don't just tell your new employee when they are supposed to be where. They're not children, after all. Help them to understand the *why* behind those expectations. It's another teaching moment, and a better way to gain commitment to the behavior you want to see. Don't just assume they know or understand. It's your job to do the work of gaining their buy-in and helping them to understand how their behavior impacts other people and the organization at large.

Questions for Reflection

- What challenges do you think your people are facing as they navigate work and life? How can you help them with that?
- How engaged are your employees with work? What steps could you take to support their engagement?
- What are your expectations for the ways that your people spend their time during the workday? How are you communicating those expectations?

4. Relationships Matter. And All My Work "Colleagues" Are Older than Me

Katherine's Experience

Let's say this together: relationships matter. As I entered the workplace for the first time, I was surprised at how easy it was to feel isolated, especially, of course, while working from home. But whether you are working remotely or not, it is still possible to go an entire day without having human interaction with someone else. You might even have interactions and *still* feel isolated and left out. If you treat your coworkers as tasks and not people, you run the risk of ending your workday with no fulfilling interactions. And this can be tempting. Not investing in relationships with your coworkers takes less effort and less time.

You are there to do a job, and I'm not saying you need to be best friends with your colleagues if you don't want to be. Different jobs require different levels of professional boundaries, and different personality types will feel more comfortable with different levels of relationships, and that is okay.

It is worth it to invest time and energy into your work relationships. Do the math! You are spending the majority of your day with these people. So get to know them and learn how to enjoy being around them.

One of the best things my mentors encouraged me to do in the first few weeks of my role was to spend twenty minutes with each person in my office, even if I didn't work directly with them or they were a few "levels" above me. I didn't think of these conversations as having an agenda or trying to network. I simply asked about the person's career experiences and how they got to where they are. As I listened, I'd ask what I was genuinely curious about. Often, this would lead to me learning about what was important in their life. They might end up talking about one of their passions, about their family, sometimes even about hobbies. If you don't have someone who encourages you to do this, take it into your own hands. Ask your new colleagues for a quick coffee or a short walk at lunch.

One thing that was new to me about making relationships in the workplace was the age gap. It was just new. I have lived my whole life placed into groups based on my age: my classrooms, my teams, my cohorts. And now, I'm just an adult, grouped in with all the other people who are 22 and older. Maybe this seems totally fine to you, and if so, great! But you also may be thinking, what if I can't find something in common with my coworkers? We are so different. I just learned how to pay the water bill and my colleague just paid off her house. Look at the list of accolades on her LinkedIn profile. Do I seem like a joke to her? Another one has young kids. Am I worth the energy it could take to get to know me?

I'll answer that last one for you: you *are* worth getting to know. I'm a strong believer that there are no uninteresting conversations, only uninterested people. So be an interest*ed* person, and you'll find interest*ing* conversation with your colleagues. And find coworkers who are interest*ed* people, and suddenly you become interest*ing*. Valuing your own story will give you the confidence you need to build some great relationships with your coworkers.

After those initial conversations, remember to continue cultivating those relationships. For me, this looked like asking my colleague about his weekend at the beginning of our call, or about her kid's school that she mentioned last week, or about what he was looking forward to for his upcoming vacation. It doesn't have to get fancy, but it does the job of making me feel connected to the people I see on a daily basis and making them feel connected to me.

It's funny. That age gap ended up being one of my favorite parts about the relationships in the workplace. Being friends with people ten, twenty, thirty years my senior was actually – get this – really FUN! My coworkers are funny, interesting, goofy, wise, caring, and thoughtful. I get to learn from them, yes, and I value their wisdom. But, most of the time, they see me and treat me as an equal, even though I have far less experience. We share jokes, stories, music recommendations. They love hearing about my roommates, my college friends, and my "adulting" fails.

All your relationships are important. Our world can sometimes suggest that relationships are just a seasoning on the meat of your accomplishments, your career, your financial success, or your ambition. Our world can also suggest that relationships are not worth the work they require. This isn't true. Relationships are valuable and essential to your life. You need other people, and they need you.

Advice for the New Professional

When Katherine outlined her thoughts for her reflection in this chapter, Allison had a good laugh at a line she included: "Becoming friends with middle-aged people is actually really FUN." That one hit a little too close to home, perhaps. Of course we're fun! As long as you don't expect us to do anything past 8 pm, and even then we have to get a sitter for the kids, figure out meals and homework, do some laundry and clean the house... never mind. We're not that fun.

As we noted in the previous chapter, a big part of figuring out life post-college is figuring out where you fit in and where you find your place. Part of that work is about where you physically fit into your community, and how you will build relationships there. You need to find some friends, yes. Some of those you will bring with you, either as roommates, or people you know in your community, or even people who now live some distance from you. And maintaining these relationships and investing in new ones will take time. As we discussed earlier, you soon will discover, if you haven't already, that you do not have a ton of free time in your life. Not only that, but that time is compressed into specific chunks at the end of the day or the end of the week.

In college it was easy to grab lunch with someone, or take a mid-day walk, or fit in other social activities around your work, because your work occupied small, discrete periods of time. You went to class for an hour and then had a break. You studied for a while and then had a break. You went to the gym, grabbed dinner, hit the library, all surrounded by your peers and friend group. But in the working world, most jobs don't act like that. Sure, things are changing, slowly, to allow for more flexibility into the workday. But for the most part, you are expected to "show up" and do work between

8-5, or even longer. That only gives you a few hours to build and maintain relationships with friends and family.

Why does this point matter? You can't maintain relationships with *everybody*. As you gain experience and knowledge about yourself, some of those people who were great friends to you in college simply won't be anymore. You just aren't meant to maintain that many relationships long-term, at that same level. You don't have time for it. Not to mention, you now are living separate lives. No longer do you wake up together, walk across campus together, go to meals together, study together. Physical separation will contribute to disconnection. And it should. Because you should be building new relationships with the people who are part of your life, now. It's time to start expanding your network beyond just your college and your high school friends. It's time to build adult relationships in this new place you're in now.

And that includes building relationships with those new work colleagues. Many, if not most (if not all) will be middle-aged or older. Like Katherine, you're not going to have a lot in common with these folks, right off the bat. You will be surrounded by people who have families and little league games and teenagers, and who are going through divorces and worrying about mortgages and a whole bunch of things that just won't seem that relevant to your life. That's OK! There's still great value in working to build relationships with these people.

Why? First, these are the people you will spend the most time with every day. There is value in collegiality, in being a good citizen of your organization. Show up to the coffee gatherings and the birthday celebrations and the volunteer events and whatever else is happening. You don't have to do everything. But people will notice your absence in these moments, which can impact your ability to be successful at work. And, second, somewhere in that group is someone who could become a mentor to you. Or a sponsor. Or a networking contact.

We all need broad, diverse networks of strong and weak ties to support our personal and professional development.[9] Who are these people? Strong ties are the people who know you well, who are always in your corner, who support you no matter what. Often these look like friends and family, but not necessarily so. The value of these people is that they are your unfailing champions and advocates. But sometimes they can have blinders on when it comes to areas that you need to improve and may not give you the feedback that you need to hear. Not always – a great strong tie is someone who both advocates for you and is honest with you – but often. Also, your strong ties usually make up a small, tight group of people, which means their ability to help you is limited and finite.

And that's why you also need weak ties. Weak ties are a few degrees out in the six degrees of separation model. Weak ties are most of the people in your LinkedIn network. They likely know you, and may even be willing to advocate for you, but they aren't necessarily going to show up for you every time you ask. Weak ties provide the benefit of access to greater opportunity and connections because each of your weak ties also has a network of their own. Weak ties can also give you more honest feedback at times because they likely don't have as much history or as deep of a relationship with you as your strong ties do.

The key is this: we all need both. The responsibility to develop these relationships rests with you. Don't sit around waiting for someone to tap you on the shoulder and give you an opportunity or take you under their wing. The important work for you to do is to seek people out, build relationships, and look for places where you can add value so that when you need it, they will want to add value to you. Many of these people will exist within your professional circles at work. So that middle-aged coworker with two kids and college tuition coming due may have more in common with your parents on a personal level, but they also have a wealth of organizational and professional knowledge and connections that can help you.

As a bonus: you might find that you like these people! Not all of them. No one ever said that you have to be best friends with the people at work, but it makes life more pleasant if you can find a friend or two there. As you get older and gain experience you'll find that you will have work friendships across the age spectrum, and that each provides value to you and to your life in different ways. This is your opportunity to start building those relationships from the beginning.[10]

Part of building an adult life is seeking out and building relationships with your peers outside of work too. Everyone needs a support system and a community. The hard part is that no one ever taught you how to make friends as a grown up. As a student you were surrounded by people your age who had similar interests and challenges. You also had a network of resources who existed to help you make friends, like residence life staff, campus life staff, planned activities both on-campus and off. And now you have to do this for yourself. How do you find friends as an adult? [11]

It's challenging, but you can do it. Essentially, you have to create those planned activities for yourself. Join groups, volunteer, put yourself in spaces where you can meet people. And, for a while at least, say yes. If someone asks you to grab coffee, say yes. If someone suggests going to a social gathering, say yes. Just like with work relationships, you don't have to be best friends with everyone. But the more you can expand your network, the greater likelihood there is that you ultimately will find those people who might get to fall into that friend category. It's not easy work. Give yourself grace and time to make it happen. With intentional work, and time, it will happen.

Questions for Reflection

- How strong is your support network? Where do you need to build relationships with more strong or weak ties?
- What steps can you take to build or deepen relationships with your colleagues?
- What steps can you take to start to build some personal relationships in your new community? How are you beginning to create some new relationships as an adult?

Advice for Managers

You might be surprised to find that one of the hardest transitions for young professionals is not from student to working professional (though that clearly does come with its own set of challenges), but from adolescence to adulthood. In fact, there is a whole body of research on this topic called "emerging adulthood."[12] We used to think about the lifespan as going from childhood immediately to adulthood, and perhaps that once was true when we used to be a largely agrarian-based society, but no more. For those of you hiring young people in their early twenties who recently graduated from college, it's important to note that they are still, in fact, in transition. Thus, the term *emerging* adulthood was developed. They are no longer children, not quite fully formed adults. Their brains aren't even fully developed yet, which has impacts on their reasoning and judgment skills and understanding of long- and short-term consequences.[13]

What does any of that have to do with you? Remember from an earlier chapter that this period of transition may impact the ways in which they show up every day to work. It doesn't let them off the hook for poor behavior, but it is an opportunity for some guidance and constructive feedback, as well as some grace from you as they inevitably screw some things up. After all, they are learning key skills right now about how to be a professional and how to be an adult in the world. These are lessons they will carry with them for the rest of their lives.

Humans are social beings by nature. We like to be in community with one another. Unless you are running some sort of cohort program with a lot of young professionals working together, there is a very good chance that, for the first time in their lives, your new employee is having to build community with people who are considerably older than they are. And possibly doing this over videoconference. This would challenge anyone, no matter their life stage.

As their manager, let's recognize that it's fair game for you to have these conversations. Talk about what community means within your organization. Allison once worked with a young professional who was pretty put off by the early morning "coffee chats" that people in the office frequently used to ease into their days, which included questions about one another's personal lives. Of course, no one should ever feel obligated to share details of their life, with you or anyone else. Sometimes it just takes explaining the "why" behind these moments. As Allison explained then, these questions weren't meant to be nosy, they were asked out of sincere interest. And the "coffee chat" time wasn't a waste, as it might have seemed on the surface, but an opportunity to build community, which pays off with work outcomes.

Everyone has things they don't enjoy doing at work and in life. Your new employee is just now figuring some of this out. People use their experiences of what they like and don't like, what gives them energy or drains them to find out where they thrive. A great conversation for you to have with them is around these experiences. Ask your new professional to reflect on what they are learning about their work environment and colleagues, as well as their own ability to show up and build relationships. Recognize that while you and others may be extroverts who enjoy social gatherings, they may be more introverted and find these experiences draining. It doesn't work for some people to do happy hour with work colleagues. Some people may have religious or family restrictions on where and how they engage in the workplace. No one should be forced to socialize in ways that infringe upon their personal choices, culture, or beliefs. Your role, as a manager, is to be an advocate for all your employees, and to build an organization that values and upholds belonging, not exclusion.

You also can be helpful by making connections for and with your new employee. Who are the people they really need to get to know within the organization, and why? Who are the people who will be great champions and supporters of their work and their forward progress? If you have the ability to make a mentoring connection, even for short-term socialization into the organization, that's great. But don't force it. Sometimes the best thing you can do for another person is to be a connector, and then get out of the way.

We all need strong networks of champions, advocates, mentors, and friends, within and outside of the workplace, no matter our experience level. As a manager, it's not your job to make every connection or introduction. At some point everyone does, in fact, need to emerge into adulthood. But as their manager there is value in remembering that they don't quite know how to do this, yet. No one shows up on day one of work knowing how to do their jobs perfectly. No one shows up on day one of life knowing how to do that perfectly, either. If anything, you should be your employee's advocate and champion, someone who wants to see them be successful both at work and in life.

Questions for Reflection

- What are the expectations or norms around "community" within your organization, and how are those upheld?
- What opportunities might your new employee be missing to build or strengthen their network?
- Who are the people you can identify to provide your new employee with mentoring, coaching, or guidance during this time of transition?

5. Setting Goals and Priorities – At Work, In Life

Katherine's Experience

It can be a challenge to figure out how to prioritize your personal and professional tasks. I group the personal and professional together because they can be difficult to separate. It *sounds* great to have one task list tracking your work tasks to complete before 5pm and one planning your personal tasks for after 5pm. But, in reality, I can be deep in thought on a work assignment while also remembering that I need to do a load of laundry for my trip this weekend. And while I'm on my lunch break, it's hard to turn off thoughts about that work project, even if I do hide my phone away for the hour. The degree to which you can balance life and work will differ from me. However, it is a balance you will have to figure out. Because, just like me, you use your same brain for all 24 hours of your day.

You'll need to decide which tasks take priority, and you need to decide when and how to accomplish them. Just this morning, when I planned to write this section of *Year One*, a more urgent task came up. So, thinking about and writing this reflection got booted to this afternoon. But would my pesky load of laundry – which still needs to get done – take precedence over the work I had planned for this morning? No, because the laundry is not urgent, and the work is important. Figuring that part out – what's urgent, what's important, what can and should be put off until later – has been a journey.

As I write this, now several months in, I realize that learning how to prioritize tasks has felt a little like an uphill battle for me this year. One tool that has worked for me is allowing my priorities to schedule my calendar in the short term. What do I mean by this? Think for a minute about your priorities this week. What's at the top of your list? Is it a looming work deadline? Making sure to call your friend? Aiming to make at least two healthy meals from home? Giving yourself 30 minutes every day to read?

Now, compare this with what your calendar tells you. If you already have an hour blocked out on your calendar to call your friend, you know you'll get it done. But if your calendar mentions nothing of your big project, other tasks could shove it out of the way, and your deadline will arrive before your project has gotten its time on your calendar. You know you need to go grocery shopping at some point this week, but you've scheduled something after work every night. It's time to say no to something before you run out of food. Is your reading goal important to you? If so, your calendar should reflect it. Don't schedule something social that ends so late every evening that you have to choose between hitting that reading goal and getting enough sleep, which is also a priority.

I'm not saying you need to be militant about your calendar. You should use whatever system or strategy works for you. These are your priorities, and no one can prioritize them for you. Here's what I am saying: there is a relationship between your time and your priorities. One will always reflect the other. But if you want to get in control of your priorities, you need to let your priorities guide your calendar not the other way around.

This same principle applies in the long run. But instead of calling it "allowing my priorities to schedule my calendar," there's a much catchier name: goal setting.

When I first started my job, Allison asked me to create a document outlining my goals for the year. I happily typed away, writing down all my hopes and dreams and aspirations for the next twelve months so that they might be spoken into existence and all come true. And then Allison gave me some feedback, which basically said, "These are great ideas, but they aren't goals." And she was right.

I think goals are often talked about as a shoot-for-the-stars exercise in dreaming as big as possible. There's a time and place for that sort of visioning. Goal setting is not it.

Goal setting is about setting a specific, targeted direction and then creating a to-do list to get there. In a classroom, you had a syllabus and a teacher to keep you on track. But in the workplace, you may be given less structure and more freedom. Setting goals ensures that your work is getting done, that it aligns with your manager's expectations, and that you are growing.

I first learned about SMART (Specific, Measurable, Achievable, Realistic, Timebound) goals in college, where they felt like busy work. In hindsight, they may have been, because I had plenty of other people making sure I was doing what I was supposed to be doing, in the right place, at the right time. At work I'm given more freedom, which also comes with expectations and responsibility. SMART goals ensure I'm meeting those expectations and upholding my responsibilities to others.

After receiving Allison's feedback, I edited my goals a bit, and now I reference that document regularly. When I need to plan out my schedule, it provides dates to follow. When I need to decide between competing priorities, it helps me decide when to say "yes" and when to say "no." When I'm feeling like I have accomplished nothing I can return to my goals and find motivation. And when I have questions about my progress I can always talk to my manager or my mentor about the goals and next steps. It's surprisingly simple and effective, and I encourage you to try it for yourself.

Advice for the New Professional

In an earlier chapter we mentioned the importance of setting some goals as you settle into those first few weeks of work. Ideally, someone – your manager – will help you to do this. In fact, you may show up to work and get handed a list of goals that you are expected to execute. While this isn't ideal – we support a collaborative process between manager and employee when creating professional goals – it is at least a clear direction for your work. Unfortunately, more often than not, you will not be given nor asked to create goals. Nor will you be provided clear direction for your work. Too often, we hear from young professionals who don't even have a clear job description. This level of uncertainty only leads to poor performance and high stress over whether or not one is doing the "right" work. It's unnecessary, but it happens.

The good news is, if this is your experience, it should not and does not prevent you from setting your own goals (or, if necessary, writing your own job description). In fact, most managers will appreciate the initiative and the opportunity to discuss your work. The reality is that most managers who don't lead this effort themselves don't know how to do it. Goal setting is one of these areas that no one teaches, and unfortunately is learned by example. If they aren't setting goals for you it's likely because no one above them does it for them, either. It's a disastrous situation for both the organization and for its people, but you can overcome it by setting your own goals.

Why should you set goals? As Katherine notes, goals define priorities. They tell you what you should be working on, and what you should not. They (should) connect to strategic direction, keeping the organization moving forward on defined metrics. They establish measures for success so that you know exactly how you will be evaluated. And, there is science to back up the value of effective goal setting, both personally and professionally. Goal setting, when it's done correctly, can change your brain, making you more motivated and likely to achieve the goal. Other research has found that when there are a lot of interests and needs competing for your attention, the simple act of creating a plan can help you not only achieve your goals but also to lessen some of the cognitive load in your brain, thus freeing up space to focus on those other needs.[14]

The limitations you have on your time as a new professional may lead to questions like these:

- How do you decide where you should and shouldn't put your focus and spend your time in your personal life?
- As you look forward towards your future, how do you identify what you should plan for, and what you shouldn't?
- As you navigate competing priorities and expectations at work, how do you figure out what you should be working on, and what you shouldn't?

Effective goal setting helps with each of these scenarios. Goal setting identifies priorities, guides decision-making, clarifies choices, and sets expectations. One of the problems with goal setting is that people often set their goals way too big or too far out into the future, creating more of a vision statement than a goal. Or, they make them too vague and have no idea how to achieve them. These are the problems with New Year's resolutions. Most people's annual resolutions look something like this: *This year, I'm going to lose thirty pounds, find my passion, and write a novel.*

These are three separate goals and should be written as such. How will you achieve each of these? What is motivating you? If you need to lose thirty pounds, what has stopped you from doing so, previously? Do those barriers still exist? What does it mean to "find your passion?" How will you know when you have found it? And, while it's certainly possible to write a novel in a year, have you written, previously? Do you have an idea? Have you created an outline?

None of these challenges posed as questions are insurmountable. The problem is, most people stop with the statement, *This year, I'm going to lose thirty pounds, find my passion, and write a novel*. And then what happens? February rolls around and no progress has been made, which leads to demotivation and the reason why most people eventually give up on their New Year's resolutions (by the second week of February, according to at least one study).[15]

The good news is, whether done professionally or personally, writing effective goal statements isn't magic, and it's something anyone can do. While there are lots of models for goal setting out there, we stand by the old standard of the SMART goal. Goals should be Specific, Measurable, Achievable, Realistic, and Timebound.

They should be Specific and start with an action verb (no starting with to be or to have), and they should be concise and to the point. If you look at your goal statement and can't define what specifically you are going to do, then you need to keep working on it. Goals should be Measurable. Try to build in a measure for success, even if you can't exactly quantify it. For example, a goal around writing a novel has as a success metric a completed draft of a novel. You either do it or you don't.

Goals should be Achievable, which means you have the resources and the ability to do the work to achieve it. It should be a stretch, but don't set yourself up for failure. And they should be Realistic, which means it is something you can and will do. Finally, they should be Timebound, which is your accountability measure. Ask yourself: when will the time come for me to look into the mirror and acknowledge whether I've accomplished my goals? When will I talk to my manager or mentors about my progress?

Once you have drafted some professional goals, bring them to your manager to discuss. This is the time to seek clarification as to whether you are focused on the right work. If they give you feedback, keep working on them! Periodically share your progress towards your goals as part of your regular one-on-one meetings. Eventually, these goals should form the basis for any performance review process, which is another reason why having clear goals are so important. If you're clear on your goals and direction, and you're in ongoing conversation with your manager about your progress, then nothing should be a surprise at performance review time (we'll discuss the importance of seeking out feedback a bit more in chapter seven).

Once you set some personal goals, which may or may not relate to your work, seek out guidance from friends, mentors, or wise counselors who can give you feedback and hold you accountable. And remember: setting goals doesn't prevent you from having dreams or from creating new ones. Setting goals isn't meant to put limitations on your life or to put you into a box. It's meant to set some priorities and bring some clarity into your life. It's a means of continually moving forward, learning and growing, and doing the work of being an adult.

Questions for Reflection

- Where do you want to be six months to a year from now?
- What are the challenges, obstacles, and gaps that may prevent you from getting there?
- What are three or four goals you can set (and commit to) for the next six months?

Advice for Managers

Effective management is centered around clear and transparent goal setting. Great managers have employees who are clear on direction, on expectations for their work and for success, and on how their work fits into the overall strategic direction of the team and the organization. The process of doing work shouldn't be a secret that someone has to figure out. Give your people direction. Communicate success metrics. No one, absolutely no one, ever did a worse job for having more information.

Setting goals with your employees also is a practice in role modeling. In talking about their goals, and helping them to write effective goal statements, you are teaching them important things about work and developing key professional (and personal!) skill sets. There is a good chance that they won't know how to do this well, because no one teaches anyone the art of writing effective goal statements. This is a gift you can give to your people. We like the SMART goal model described in the previous pages, because it's clear and simple, and when done well it results in effective, usable goal statements and action steps. You might have another system that works for you, that's fine. What's important is that the goals get written and that they get used.

Goals aren't meant to sit in a drawer. Too many managers and organizations spend inordinate amounts of time (which is, at the end of the day, money) putting their people through exercises to create vision and mission statements, goals and success metrics, and then never ask about them or hold people accountable for the work. If you're going to do the work of goal setting, and you should, then you should actually use them. Every time you have a regular one-on-one with your employees, check in on their goals and their progress, find out what's challenging them or preventing them from being successful, and find out how you can help.

Another benefit to goal setting is that it helps with determining priorities and making decisions, skill sets that every employee needs to develop but few have in great supply on day one of a new job. It can be challenging to figure out which work projects take priority, which directive from higher-ups should be followed, or how much time should be allotted to any given work assignment. Great managers build in these conversations with their employees. Don't make your people have to guess what you want or when you want it. Give clear deadlines and set clear expectations through the goals that you set with your employees.

Begin your working relationship by having open conversations about how much work assignments should take, and why. Many young professionals express frustration because their manager gives them an assignment with the (unstated) expectation that they spend several days completing it, and the new employee is able to do that work within hours. Perhaps the manager is under-valuing the young professional's skill set. Or, perhaps there is a reason the manager wanted it to take several days and the new professional, in their speed to get the assignment completed, has missed some key steps and a clear understanding of the bigger picture.

Goal setting also connects to the feedback process, which we will discuss more in chapter seven. Think about how you are using regular goal setting as part of your feedback and annual review processes. No one should get to annual review time and not know how they will be evaluated. No one should ever wonder what they should be working on, or why. That's your job, as the manager: to set and communicate clear expectations, and to hold people accountable for their work.

If, as a manager, you are regularly checking in on your employees and the work they are doing, having open conversations about their progress towards their goals and how you can help support them, then you should not need for them to write up a summary of what they have been working on all year in their annual review. Great performance reviews are truly reflective.[16] They should be an opportunity for both employee and manager to think about what went well, what has been learned, and how you and they can use that knowledge in the future to continue growing and developing in their roles.

Setting goals is a first step towards effective performance reviews. You set goals together with your employees at the beginning of the year, which clarifies direction and expectations. You check in on a regular basis and adjust the goals as needed throughout the year. You provide ongoing feedback on the work so that the employee can continue to grow in their skills and knowledge. And then, when you get to the annual review, the goals set the framework for the review conversation, and the progress and the ongoing feedback provides the content for the conversation. It should all connect together.

Finally, make sure that your employees have up-to-date versions of their job descriptions. Far too often we hear from young professionals who are several years into a role and trying to negotiate for a raise or a promotion yet have never seen a job description. This is an unacceptable human resource management practice, a liability for you as a manager, and simply not a good way to treat people. Give your people what they need. Set them up for success, support them as they do the work, and you'll be amazed by the results you get.

Questions for Reflection

- How are you communicating goals, priorities, and work expectations to your employee?
- What are the measures of success for performance?
- How are you building in regular feedback conversations with your employees on their work and progress towards their goals?

6. Who Let Me in Here?

Katherine's Experience

After I graduated, I found answering the question, "tell me about yourself," more difficult. For most of my life, I had responded with things like what I liked to do in my free time, where I grew up, as well as my most significant identity: "I am a student." Sometimes, more specifically: "I am an English major," or, "I am a student at Wake Forest University." Regardless, when I walked into a classroom, a networking event, or a family reunion, my identity was almost entirely about my personal and professional role as a college student.

Now, I find myself in my first workplace with an expired student ID still in my wallet, needing different words to describe who I am and what matters to me. It's sometimes challenging to find the words that allow me to claim my voice and my space, to claim this new professional identity. Finding your place and voice in the workplace often involves answering questions such as the following:

- What do I bring to the table?
- What are my strongest skills?
- Where do I need to grow or ask for help?
- How do my skills fit into the skills of the others in my workplace?

On my most focused days I could answer these questions and even present myself well to my colleagues and others. But on a lot of days, when I was practicing a new skill, or when I couldn't see my coworker's reaction because we were working from home, it was really easy to believe that I didn't belong. It was easy to convince myself that I had no clue what I was doing. It was easy to remember that I was the youngest person in the room; therefore, there was no point in speaking up, because who was I to add to this conversation?

I've talked about this self-doubt before. And not only is it a difficult personal and internal experience, it's also one that can affect your external behavior, your relationships, and your ability to be successful at work.

This struggle to find my own voice at work was a complete surprise to me. I didn't even think about it before I graduated, because I didn't realize how important it would be to my personal and professional growth to find a confident voice at work. But after a few weeks into my job, I realized that I was withholding my thoughts far too often in meetings, which was something I had not done in my previous life as a student.

One of the best things I did when I realized this was happening was to ask my mentor and managers how to get better at this, which went something like this: "I wish I were more confident to speak up during meetings, but I often doubt myself. How would you recommend I grow in this? Did you ever experience something similar in a new role?"

I received a slew of personal and practical advice to help. My mentor (and co-author) reminded me that I have valuable and necessary ideas worth contributing. In meetings we were in together, she opened space for me to practice sharing my thoughts and building self-confidence. Her belief in me helped me believe in myself.

Another one of my managers suggested a few practices to try out. It was helpful for me to hear that even a high-achieving professional had to jot down his comments before sharing it in a meeting. I've picked up this practice as well (and felt less embarrassed to do so). He reminded me to take all opportunities I can when they present themselves, and this has helped me to find confidence to speak up even when it's not the "perfect" moment. He also reminded me of ways to take advantage of a virtual work environment. When I'm feeling shy in a Zoom meeting, I can throw a comment in the chat rather than saying it aloud or share something on Slack if I'm nervous to send out an email to the team. These low-risk opportunities were some of the entryways to my own discovery of my voice and claiming my space.

What does your voice sound like right now? What would you like it to sound like? Is it hesitant to speak up? Is it assertive and confident? Who are the trusted mentors, managers, colleagues, and role models in your workplace or life who can help you to find your voice? Give yourself grace to make some mistakes as you practice using your voice. You were hired for a reason. You were invited into the room for a reason. Remind yourself of this when those doubts start to creep in and encourage yourself to speak up when you might stay silent.

Advice for the New Professional

One of the most challenging parts of starting any new role, and especially your first role in the working world, is getting over that feeling that you have no idea what you're doing. To some extent, this feeling is valid: you *don't* know what you're doing, and you shouldn't, because you're new and this is your first professional role after graduation. It's fine to embrace that feeling and to acknowledge it. In fact, you may have been given or heard the advice to "fake it 'til you make it." While there can be some value in this, and we all do it from time to time, we would like to steer you away from this mindset for now.

As we have discussed in an earlier chapter, there actually is great value in being the new person. You get to ask the questions others don't feel like they can ask anymore. You get to add a valuable, fresh new perspective! You don't have to feign ignorance because you actually are ignorant about a lot of things. And, let's be honest: those people who are truly "faking it" may think they are pulling something over on other people, when in fact it's actually quite obvious to everyone that they don't know what they are talking about. The people who hired you have seen your resume, they know what your experience is. Not a single person there is under the impression that you walked in the door on day one with fifteen years of experience in the field and a Ph.D. Pretending to be something you're not makes you look foolish, and can burn relationships and trust with your manager and your colleagues. (Sidenote, this is also why you should not pretend to be something you are not in an interview setting. Yes, be professional and polished. But if you pretend to be something you are not, and then get hired, well, you're going to have to maintain that facade for a very long time. And you could get fired for it.)

At the same time, it's important to recognize when you truly don't know what you're doing versus when you are experiencing a bit of impostor syndrome. What is impostor syndrome? It's the very common experience of questioning your worth, of feeling like you have somehow snuck in a side door when no one was looking and soon will be found out.[17] It's the feeling that everyone else but you somehow knows the rules and norms of behavior and how to be successful in this place. It shows up when you don't apply for a job because you don't have every single qualification listed on the job description. Or when you don't put yourself forward for a leadership position because you can't see yourself as a leader. Or when you don't speak up in a meeting and claim your voice.

We all experience the feeling of being an impostor now and again. It sometimes can break on gender or race lines – women can tend to feel it more than men, people of color more than white people – but that's not because women or people of color are less qualified or capable. It's because we (white, cisgender, people of privilege) have created systems and structures of oppression that make women and people of color feel less qualified or capable. This is one of the very real impacts of organizations focusing on diversity but not taking the steps to build cultures of inclusion where all people feel that they belong and can be successful. When organizations open the doors to Black, LGBTQ, female, neurodiverse, and other individuals, but do not create the systems and structures that elevate their voices and their experiences and provide opportunities for advancement, it leads to self-doubt and devaluing their experiences, if not outright harmful behaviors of bias, discrimination, and racism. That's not impostor syndrome, that's organizations blaming the individual instead of looking for ways to improve the organization.[18] If you find yourself in this situation, your first step is to talk to your manager or a trusted mentor and then to seek out guidance from human resources. No one should be made to feel less than capable or deserving of opportunities based on who they are.

Now, let it be noted, feeling like an impostor does not give you license not to do your homework to figure out how to do your job. It's time to become very clear on what your strengths and capabilities are and recognize how to put them to work. For example, you may be in an organization or an industry that uses a lot of acronyms. You are perfectly capable of looking those up and learning them, and you should. Or, if you aren't provided an onboarding process that clearly explains norms and expectations of behavior, you need to do the homework to figure those things out. If your manager doesn't give you goals, then you need to do the work to create some, as we discussed in the previous chapter. None of this is about feeling like an impostor. It's about being a rock star professional who takes initiative.

When impostor syndrome rears its ugly head, you do have some tools at your disposal to help you to get through it. One of the best tools is to find those mentors and wise counselors who can give you the advice and feedback that you need. There is great research out there demonstrating the power of connection to other people's experiences and stories as a strategy for getting through impostor syndrome.[19] And since almost everyone goes through it at one point or another, there are a lot of people and stories available to help you!

We will talk about feedback a bit more in the next chapter. For now, let's think about how you start to build that network of support that is going to help you. The good news is, you've already done the important work of setting some goals for yourself, which is step number one to building a strong network. You've identified those strong and weak ties, and probably found some gaps you need to fill too, which is step number two. So now we come to the part where you need to identify the people who can help you to fill those gaps to work towards achieving your goals.

Mentoring has become a popular term in recent years, so much so that it is easy to throw it around as the be-all, end-all fix to every problem. This is not how you should approach building your network. First, let's recognize what mentoring is. As we define it, effective mentoring is a purposeful and personal relationship in which a more experienced person (mentor) provides guidance, feedback, and wisdom to facilitate the growth and development of a less experienced person (mentee). Mentoring relationships are in-depth commitments, both to the other person and to the work that is to be done. They are focused on the learning and growth of the mentee, and about forward action to achieve identified learning goals. When stated that way, you might be thinking, "Sounds nice, but that's not really what I need or want right now."

That's great! Not everyone in your network should rise to the level of a mentoring relationship, just like not everyone in your network is going to rise to the level of being a strong tie. Sometimes what you need is more of a wise counselor, who is someone who can give you some advice and guidance in the moment based on their experience, but without that relationship commitment. Or, at some point you might need more of a sponsor, someone who can and will advocate for you to higher ups for opportunities and promotions. At times, all you need is a networking contact. The bottom line is that you have to do the work to figure out what you need, and then you do the work to build those relationships.

When faced with moments of impostor syndrome, a mentor can be quite useful. Early on in your role, when you've yet to build these relationships with your new professional colleagues, you might look to people you already know. Who are the people you asked to serve as a reference for you when you were applying to the job? Who are your go-to people for advice and guidance when faced with a challenging decision point? Start there.

As you start to build relationships with your new colleagues, look for the people who can serve as those wise counselors. Expecting anyone to jump into a formal mentoring relationship with you right off the bat is a big ask. Remember: they are all dealing with their own stuff and may not have a lot of time or energy to worry about yours. But asking someone to grab coffee for fifteen minutes, so that you can benefit from the wisdom of their experience, is a much lower ask of someone's time.

Think about where these impostor feelings are coming from. Is it your relationships with your new colleagues? Look for someone who seems to have built strong relationships based on trust. Is it a work project that feels beyond your capabilities? Seek out a colleague you trust for advice on delivering a successful outcome. In an ideal world, talk to your manager about what you're feeling. But let us add a note of caution here. Your manager is not necessarily your mentor and doesn't see themselves that way. Ultimately this is the person responsible for evaluating you and your work. If that doesn't feel like a safe place for sharing your vulnerability and challenges, then don't do it.

At a certain point, you need to acquire the ability to assess your own strengths and growth opportunities, which is part of building your emotional intelligence, or EQ, which we will discuss in the following chapter. As you grow in your career, you should not constantly need other people to pump you up and tell you that you deserve to be in the room. So when you are struggling, remind yourself of this truth: no one ever gave someone a job out of pity. You deserve to be there. You were given a place in the room based on your skills and your strengths. Now it's up to you to figure out how to use them.

Questions for Reflection

- What does your voice sound like right now? Is it meek and cautious or confident and assertive? What would you like it to sound like?
- When does impostor syndrome show up for you? What strategies have helped you to navigate through it in the past?
- Who are trusted mentors, colleagues, wise counselors, and role models in your workplace or life who can help you to find your voice and work through impostor syndrome?

Advice for Managers

Think back to your first professional experience. Did you feel like you belonged from day one? Did you feel like an expert and like you knew what you were doing? Probably not. Everyone suffers from impostor syndrome now and again. It's not unique to young professionals. Every time someone takes on a new role, or joins a new organization, or tackles a new assignment, there is the opportunity to feel like a new person again, and, like the title to this chapter suggests, to question, who let me in here? You may have felt it the first time you took on the role of manager. It's normal. In fact, *not* experiencing a bit of impostor syndrome from time to time is far more concerning. What's not normal, or healthy, is to stay in this mindset for an extended period. It will start to impact your ability to be productive and effective.

There's a pretty good chance your new employee is suffering a bit from impostor syndrome right now, which might show up in one of two ways. One, they can adopt a mode of timidity, not daring to speak up or share their opinion, constantly seeking out feedback and affirmation, and prefacing their statements with things like, "I may be wrong, but...," or, "I don't know what I'm talking about, but..." Or, two, they can try to cover with exaggerated bravado, trying to do everything on their own, not asking questions when they should, and seeming to "know-it-all" and brush off suggestions or offers for help. Either approach will be harmful to them if left unchecked.

In the first case, it's important for you as the manager to pull the employee aside and make note of where they are hesitating when they should not be. Identify the moments that they use self-deprecating or self-defeating language and how it lands in the room. Point out their skills and strengths and how they can use them to add value to their work projects and colleagues. Encourage them in the moment by asking for their opinion. Everyone needs affirmation now and again. But if they are seeking it constantly and unnecessarily, that is a conversation you need to have with them.

In the second case, it's also important for you to pull the employee aside and talk about their behavior. Make note of the times where they seem to want to go it alone instead of inviting in other perspectives and advice from their more-experienced colleagues. Openly discuss how this sort of behavior can impact and is impacting their work. Point out places where they should be asking questions before charging forward. Remind them that you want them to be successful and discuss how these types of behaviors can stall or even derail their career long-term.

We know that young people entering the workforce right now are seeking out mentorship, feedback, skill development, career advancement, and connection to meaningful work.[20] For many managers, this can feel like the hallmarks of an entitled young professional. But think about it: what do you want from work? Probably, mentorship, feedback, skill development, career advancement, and meaningful work. These are universal desires and needs across the workforce. These young people are just brave enough to ask for it. And, they are brave enough to leave and find work elsewhere, if and when they realize they aren't getting these things from you.

So, what can you do to be helpful? Give regular, objective feedback. Look for opportunities where you can intentionally and strategically grow their skills and confidence through work assignments and discuss how that is happening. Talk to your employee (to all your employees) about where they see their career going, long-term, and how this work connects to those goals and how they find meaning and purpose. Make it OK for them to look for those opportunities, elsewhere, when that time comes. The reality is, they may leave you one day down the road. But they're far more likely to do so if you're *not* having these conversations, than if you are.

As a manager, you can adopt strategies of mentorship into your management style, which include getting to know your employees as individuals, helping them to set and work towards developmental goals, providing ongoing and objective feedback, and setting and communicating clear expectations for success. These are strategies which will make you more effective as a manager and help to build a culture of growth and development on your team. But that doesn't mean you should serve in a role of formal mentor to your people; in fact, this can often do more harm than good. True mentors need to be able to hear their mentees' challenges and struggles and failures without passing judgment on them. This is a tall order for anyone who is ultimately going to write someone's performance review and make decisions on raises and promotions.

But what you can and should do is help your people find great mentors, sponsors, and others who can help them to work through professional and personal challenges and goals, and that includes navigating impostor syndrome. If your employee is struggling to find their place or to find confidence in their abilities, help them to identify someone who has worked through that and who can share their story in a confidential space. It will help your employee grow in their skills and build community, it will help the employee serving as a mentor to grow in their skills and understanding of others' experiences, and ultimately it will help you, as a manager, too.

Finally, as we noted in the previous section, there is a very real difference between an individual working through a bit of impostor syndrome and an organization that uses it as an excuse not to build a culture of inclusion and belonging. Your job, as a manager, is to make sure that all your employees feel heard, feel valued, and have opportunities to grow and develop in their careers based solely on their performance, skills, and abilities, and not on their identities. Your job is not to "fix people," it's to create a healthy, inclusive organization that values diverse experiences and voices.

Questions for Reflection

- When might your employee experience impostor syndrome? How does it show up in their behavior and language?
- What strategies can you share for helping the employee to claim their place and their voice?
- Where can you build in intentional developmental conversations with your employee?

7. Nobody Gets an "A" in Life

Katherine's Experience

As a kid, I dreamed sometimes of having school with no grades. It seemed like total freedom, play, and no stress. Imagine what school actually would have been like! No measures of growth, no awareness of opportunities to do better. My teachers could have been totally disappointed in me and I'd have had no idea. I could have been miles behind my peers and not even know. No success metrics sounds great in the very short term, but pretty soon, I would have been second guessing myself all the time, constantly wondering if I had the approval of those who matter, just hoping and praying that I would end up on track or ahead of my peers in five years.

Well... without the right tools, that's kind of what the working world is like. There's not a uniform, written standard for success, and certainly no gradebook or syllabi to follow. But don't worry! There are ways to succeed and thrive in this new structure, it just takes a little readjusting.

To be honest, I wasn't really prepared for this change. Until I learned a few lessons, I did a lot of second-guessing of myself. Sometimes I asked myself if I was doing too much, but I most often asked myself if what I was doing was good enough (again, that impostor syndrome rearing its head). It was hard to determine what "good work" looked like and how to make sure I was on track.

My first lesson was realizing that I didn't have to ask myself these questions. Because, duh! I needed to ask my manager, the person who *does* know the answers. And when I realized this, I began to take seriously what my mentor and managers had been telling me since I started working: asking for feedback and guidance is important, and you are capable of doing it well even though it sometimes can be scary to do so.

The second lesson I learned came from the mentor of my roommate. Just like me, she was doubting herself and her abilities. Her mentor helped to connect the dots between this self-doubt and the lack of clearly communicated expectations in a workplace, and the important individual work of figuring out how, and to whom, to hold yourself accountable. He advised us to "discern when others are yelling at you, and when you're yelling at yourself." In other words, sometimes we hold ourselves to self-imposed standards of "perfection" that are both unreasonable and unwarranted. My roommate and I have chosen to hold this saying as a proverb of our twenties, something we return to time and again, and I share it here in case it helps you, too.

Advice for the New Professional

One of the unexpected differences between college and work and life after college is the clear structure and defined expectations of school and the lack of structure and lack of expectations at work and in life. As the title of this chapter notes, nobody gets an "A" in life, because there is no such thing. While you might have a sense of what "success" in life looks like, it's entirely subjective and you get to define it. And while we hope that your organization or your manager provides you with clear parameters for success at work, you should understand by now that this may not happen, either. You no longer exist in the world of syllabi and immediate feedback. For many young professionals, this lack of guidance is unsettling and takes some getting used to.

Just because you want something, such as career advancement, doesn't mean that you will get it. But that does not mean you don't deserve coaching, feedback, and guidance on your path. There is no reason why you should know everything there is to know about being successful within your organization, or your life, on day one. This isn't innate knowledge that you were born with. But that doesn't let you off the hook for doing the work you need to do to figure it out. You have to seek out the feedback and guidance that you need to be successful, and eventually gather the information, the tools, and the resources that you need to do this work for yourself.

Doing that work is part of what's called developing your emotional intelligence or your EQ, and it's incredibly important. In fact, some research has argued that EQ accounts for up to 58 percent of job performance and is the "strongest driver of leadership and personal excellence."[21] (It's worth noting that other research has disputed these figures.[22]) Being smart and talented helps. But it's EQ, not how naturally smart or gifted you are, that's ultimately going to help you to be successful during these first few years and long-term. So, what is it and how do you do it?

EQ is "your ability to recognize and understand emotions in yourself and others and your ability to use this awareness to manage your behavior and relationships." [23] Or, to put it another way, it is your ability to navigate interpersonal relationships, build networks, and manage your emotions and behaviors. Have you ever thought to yourself, "That person has no social skills?" That person to whom you're referring is likely low in EQ. Or, you may find yourself working for or with someone who struggles to build rapport and trust with their colleagues. That person is low in EQ.

EQ has four components: [24]

- **Self-awareness:** your ability to recognize your emotions and mood and how it impacts others.
- **Self-management:** your ability to manage your impulses and moods, and to think before acting or reacting.
- **Social awareness:** your ability to gauge accurately the emotions of others through listening and observing.
- **Relationship management:** your ability to build rapport, build networks, and to inspire trust.

Fortunately, your EQ can and should be developed. Here are a few tips for you to try to get started:

- **Pay attention to your emotional, verbal, and physical responses.** Write down your responses to different experiences. What patterns do you start to notice? When do you get frustrated or find your mood is impacted by the behavior of others?
- **Practice not responding.** The next time you have the urge to jump in and argue a point, try taking a step back. What were you going to say and why? What was the result of you not making yourself heard?
- **Seek out feedback.** Ask a trusted friend or colleague to observe you in different situations and to give you feedback on how you engage with others and how you manage your own responses. Try to resist the urge to defend yourself, but simply listen and ask questions for clarification, and then reflect on what you heard.

The last chapter was all about those critical relationships you need to develop with people who can support you as you develop your EQ, get over impostor syndrome, and start to identify your strengths and growth opportunities. This work takes time! It's a lifelong, ongoing process. By asking for feedback, not over-reacting to it emotionally, and taking their input seriously, you continue to do the work of building those relationships.

Another critical component to this EQ work is building what is known as a "growth mindset." This phrase was coined by Stanford researcher Carol Dweck, and refers to the belief system, *the mindset*, needed to stay open to learning, to moving forward in one's life, to overcoming adversity, and working through change.[25] It's a necessary ingredient for forward progress, both personally and professionally. A fixed mindset is one that says, "I'll never learn how to do this job well, so why even bother to try?" A growth mindset says, "I've got a lot to learn in order to do this job well, but I'm willing to do the work and to try." A growth mindset is a necessary element for successful career development. We are each a mixture of both growth and fixed mindsets. Your job is to constantly work to flex those growth mindset muscles, to stay in a place of learning, adapting, and listening.

As you begin to set personal and professional goals for yourself, the information that people share with you and what you are learning about yourself will provide critical data points that will help you begin to define what "success" means for you. Expect that definition to change over time as you gain clarity on what matters to you. Nobody gets an "A" in life, not in the sense to which you are accustomed. But the good news is, you get to decide what an "A" life looks like, for you, and then do the work to create it.

Questions for Reflection

- Where are your EQ gaps and what steps can you take to start to fill them?
- When are you most likely to adopt a growth mindset? How can you do more of that?
- How are you defining success for yourself right now?

Advice for Managers

In the last chapter we discussed helping your employees work through impostor syndrome as they find their footing in this uncertain transition from college student to new professional. And, as we mentioned, it's important to point out those moments where they either aren't giving themselves enough credit, or perhaps are giving themselves too much credit for knowing what they are doing. These are important conversations and shouldn't be one-time conversations. They are all part of the feedback process that will help your new employee to learn how to be a professional.

As an experienced working adult, it's important to take a moment and put yourself in your young employee's shoes for a moment. There is no reason why they should know how to do this well. For many young employees, literally nothing in their life up to this moment has looked like, or prepared them, for this. They have spent sixteen-plus years on academic schedules, sitting in classrooms with their peers, taking courses with identified start and end dates as well as clear measures for success. At least twice a year they have been able to begin again with a clean slate. We believe in education, and we believe in college education for how it prepares people to think critically, communicate well, work in teams, and gain deep knowledge in a variety of subjects. But from a process standpoint, there is nothing about college, or the educational system as a whole, that prepares anyone for the process of work or for life. If they are lucky, they will have had prior work experience with developmental feedback built into that experience. But many will not have had this, before, and they will be looking to you for guidance.

You may not feel like this is your job. But it is. The moment you decided to take on this new employee, you agreed to teach them something about work and life, whether you realized it or not. Every day you will teach them about what acceptable and successful professional behavior looks like in the ways that you show up, the ways that you communicate, and the ways that you treat your people. It will come through in the ways that you deal with success and failure. Whether you intend it or not, people will be paying

attention, and they will notice. Unlike your more experienced employees, this new professional lacks the context or the wisdom to discern what "acceptable" behavior looks like. So, if you are not talking to them about it, just know that they are equating your behavior with successful management and leadership. And that has long-lasting impacts.

You can make the choice to have intentional, ongoing conversations with your new employee about how they are figuring out work, what they are learning along the way, how they are using and building upon their strengths and growing and developing their weaknesses. You can give regular, ongoing feedback on how they are showing up to work, how they are interacting with their new colleagues, how they are performing, and why it matters.

They learned how to be a student through sixteen-plus years of scaffolded learning and skills. No one asked them to do college-level writing in elementary school. Allison's father is a seventh-grade language arts teacher and one of the assignments his students have to do is to learn how to write a "perfect paragraph." The perfect paragraph leads to the essay which leads to the research paper which eventually leads to college-level writing. But it starts with the paragraph, not the twenty-page paper.

You should think about work the same way. What will your new employee need to know how to do a year from now, and how can you start to implement the building blocks for that, now? Think about scaffolding skills through intentional experiences and then have accompanying conversations about what they are learning, and why. Sure, it's a lot of work. It's an investment of time. It might feel like your new employee needs a lot of coaching and feedback, and they do. But that's what you signed up for when you decided to become a people manager. If you don't want to do the work, then you should think about giving that opportunity to someone else.

Feedback conversations can be challenging because no one teaches this skill set to managers, or anyone else. We put people into roles where they are responsible for the work (and ultimately the livelihoods) of other people, and then provide them with zero training or coaching on how to do that well. What results is a lot of frustration, and hurt feelings, and at the very least poor morale and poor work. If you want to know why your young people are "jumping ship," ask yourself:

- Did I provide meaningful work that connected to their goals and purpose?
- Did I talk to them about their growth and progress?
- Did I provide regular, ongoing feedback that helped them to learn?

Here is our favorite feedback model. Feedback should be immediate, objective, and impactful. It should be immediate and delivered as close in time as possible to the behavior being addressed. That doesn't mean that as soon as you have a thought you should say it out loud. Sometimes there is value in sleeping on it and gathering additional information. At the same time, this is one of the problems with "annual" performance reviews. If you're only giving people feedback once a year, you're missing a lot of opportunities for growth and learning.

Feedback should be objective, which means that it should be based on observed behaviors and actions as much as possible. And lastly, it should be impactful, demonstrating impact on yourself, on the other person, or on others. For example: *Yesterday, in our team meeting, when you were on your phone, you made your colleagues feel like you didn't value their time or contributions.* This statement is immediate (yesterday), based on objective, observed behavior (you were on your phone in our meeting), and demonstrates the impact of that behavior (your colleagues felt devalued).

It's also important to remember that feedback doesn't also have to be, nor should it always be critical in nature. We need to catch people doing great things, too. You want to use the same model for positive feedback. Telling someone, "You're awesome!" might feel better, to you and to them, but it doesn't help with growth. How are they awesome? In what specific ways have you observed them being awesome, and how did it impact others, so that they might repeat that behavior in the future?

Feedback should always be about growth and learning. Keep your people in front of you, stay focused on their growth, and you will give them the feedback they deserve.

Questions for Reflection

- What does your behavior demonstrate about being a successful adult professional?
- How are you scaffolding skills through intentional professional learning experiences?
- When was the last time you had an intentional feedback conversation?

8. Navigating Politics. Or, Why Don't Grown Ups Act Like Grown Ups?

Katherine's Experience

Ooof. Organizational politics. Let's throw that at the top of the list of things I didn't know I needed to think about when I entered my first year of work. I'm really lucky to work in a place with a positive culture, but that doesn't mean it doesn't have its challenges. Learning how to navigate politics is something I have done alongside my roommates, friends, and even family members as they, too, experience the unique complexities of their own organizations.

It surprised me to find out that just like any other community – your family, your favorite club in college, your religious community – your workplace also includes complex relationships that experience growth and conflict. Depending on your workplace culture and personal boundaries, this could take on different forms, but everyone brings their emotions, values, and opinions to work.

Your workplace culture will be made up of all the personalities within it, for better or for worse. Some organizational behaviors will be self-serving. Some of your colleagues may act in certain ways or befriend certain people to gain positive outcomes within the organization. I'm not here to tell you when that's right or when that's wrong, so I would implore you to find a trusted friend or co-worker with whom you feel safe processing your reactions to these dynamics. It can help you to better understand and digest these new interpersonal dynamics that you may never have encountered previously.

It helped me to learn and understand the interpersonal dynamics of my office in order to effectively manage my own workday, even though at times it felt like a burden. It also helped to learn and understand (to a lesser extent) the interpersonal dynamics of my roommates' and friends' offices, who were getting to know their organizations as I was getting to know mine. These conversations took me outside my own organization and helped me see the bigger picture. It helped me to understand that every office, every organization, behaves differently and upholds different values and norms, which is all part of the experience of working there and being successful there.

So, while I entered into my first role unprepared to navigate organizational politics, I've grown in confidence slowly as I have held each interpersonal situation as a lesson to learn rather than an experience to dread. If a situation is brand new to me, it means that I get to move it from the "I've never faced this before" shelf down to the more-accessible "I've navigated this before" shelf. The more crowded that bottom shelf is, the more well-equipped you'll be in your career moving forward.

Advice for the New Professional

Figuring out organizational culture and organizational politics can be one of the most important things you do at work. It can be energizing to learn that you are in a place that aligns with your values and strengths. It can be uplifting to know that you are part of a team of people who are all working towards the same goal. And occasionally it can be frustrating and a bit disappointing. Why? Because workplaces are filled with people, and people are messy, and just because people are grown-ups, it doesn't mean they are going to act that way. Adults can be gossipy, they can be petty, they can hold grudges and build cliques. Working with adults can often feel like working with a bunch of pre-teens who get caught up in power plays and silly arguments that have nothing to do with the actual work. Not all of them are like this, of course. But it happens, and when it does, it impacts the work. It can impact your work.

One of the biggest clues to organizational culture can be found in what gets rewarded, and what doesn't. Every organization is different, and it's worth it for you to take some time to pay attention to what does get rewarded in yours. Take note of the following:

- Who gets to attend meetings?
- Who gets to have a voice?

- Who gets promoted and why?
- When there is bad behavior, what happens?
- When someone makes a mistake, what happens?

Every organization has a culture. And those cultures are created by the people who work there. Toxic work cultures – cultures that are built on demeaning, shaming, bullying behaviors – aren't inherent to the organization. These things exist because the people who make up the organization act in demeaning, shaming, and bullying ways, and that behavior is either upheld or, worse, rewarded. And the same goes for the opposite. A supportive culture built upon growth and development comes from the people. It's not about the actual work getting done, or where that work happens. It's about how it gets done and how it happens, what gets rewarded and how people are held accountable.

You have to learn how to read organizational culture. You will learn, with time, that this is one of the most important factors in your ability to be successful, to enjoy your work, and to start to build a career that has meaning and purpose to you. It's easy, when you're just starting out, to put all your focus on the work tasks: *I want to work in finance*, or, *I want to be a teacher*, or, *I want to do client strategy*. This process is not unimportant. Not everyone is well-suited to be an investment banker or a teacher or a marketer. But you also (presumably) want to do that work within an environment that supports your growth, that motivates you and challenges you, and that ultimately aligns with who you are. And this is built by the people with whom you will spend all day, every day.

Take some time during this first year to learn the culture of your organization and pay particular attention to the stated values and those that are lived out every day. For example, your organization may have a stated value (these usually can be found on the website) of upholding principles of diversity, equity, and inclusion. But in actual practice, you may notice that the people in your organization are mainly white, cisgender, and male, and those who fall outside of those groups do not feel included in decision-making processes. What, then, does that say about the actual culture of the organization?

In addition to learning to read the culture, you have to learn how to play politics effectively. At the end of the day, you may not love everything about the culture of your organization, but you probably lack the organizational capital to make significant change to it, at this point. But that doesn't mean you can't be successful in your role or organization. Part of reading the culture is determining who the people are who hold the power and the influence. Those are the people you want to bring into your network (as long as it doesn't compromise your own values). Identify the people who can champion your work and make sure it gets uplifted and accomplished. And identify those who can impact your ability to be successful.

This is what playing politics looks like. In very few organizations does work get accomplished alone. It is done through and with people, and you need to figure out who those people are and how to effectively work with them. You will learn what happens when you don't invite certain people into a project planning discussion. Or what happens if you don't seek approval from certain people, even if it feels like they have nothing to do with your work.

Another version of playing politics is learning how to engage with certain people. Take some time to figure out other peoples' motivations. Some are motivated by power and control. You always want to make them feel like they get the final word. Others are motivated by safety and security, so you want to reassure them that in no way are you a threat to them or their position. Some see themselves as the "coach," and even if you don't, when you interact with them you want to make them feel like you have something to learn from them.

This can all feel pretty icky at first, and like something you shouldn't have to do just to get your work done. And you're right, you shouldn't. You shouldn't have to play games at work just to get your work done. Adults shouldn't act this way. But they do, and if you want to be successful, you have to learn how to play the game successfully. Of course, you should never compromise your own values and integrity for your job. Ever. And since work is always about relationships, learning how to manage your relationships with others effectively is key to your ability to be successful.

- What have you learned about your organization's culture? What are those norms and organizational values that get upheld? What gets rewarded and what doesn't?
- Who are the most important people in your organization and who are the least important, and how are the people in each of those groups treated?
- Where are the gaps between the stated values of the organization, and the actual lived values on a day-to-day basis? How do you feel about that?

Advice for Managers

Organizational culture is one of the most fascinating and important elements to work-life that we encounter. Organizations have values, just like individuals do. Your organization might have a set of stated values on a wall or on a website. And, more than likely, your organization has a set of practiced values that may or may not align with those stated values. As a manager, it's important for you to pay attention to the actual, lived values of your organization and whether those behaviors are the ones you want reinforced or uplifted.

There's an old saying that "what gets measured is what gets done." In a similar fashion, what gets rewarded are the behaviors that will be reinforced. If you, as a manager, are constantly talking about the importance of collaborative team work, but promote and lift up those who bully and step on their colleagues to get ahead, then what the organization hears and sees is that it's every person for themselves. On the other hand, if you consistently call out collaborative work and actively reward it, those will be the behaviors that get reinforced.

Organizations, then, can be both healthy and toxic. Healthy cultures grow and support people, provide clear expectations for success, reward good behavior and correct negative behavior, and build inclusion and belonging for all employees. Toxic cultures do the opposite. It's not about money, although certainly everyone wants to be fairly compensated for their work. But if it was just about the money, then non-profits would have the most toxic cultures and corporate entities would have the healthiest, and that's not at all the case.

As we noted in the preceding pages, one of the most jarring transitions for young employees is the realization that adults quite frequently don't act like grown-ups. Even as they have been inching towards adulthood, these young people have still been in environments where the "grown-ups" occupied positions of authority and power, deserved or not. When they graduate and move out into the workforce, young adults get a first-hand look at how decisions get made, how people hold onto or share power, and the other elements that make up organizational culture and work. And it's not always pretty.

The good news is that these topics are great mentoring moments and management conversations for you. Spend some time talking to your new employee about organizational culture, both the culture of your own organization and also why culture matters. Now, the idea of "culture fit" has become a pretty loaded term over recent years because, in interviewing terms, it can be a proxy for bias (i.e., "he/she/they aren't a good fit here," is used when people actually mean, "he/she/they aren't white enough/ straight enough/male enough" etc.). Any time this term comes up in hiring (or firing) decisions it should be immediately questioned.

But from the new employee's side, culture fit is important. These are great questions for all employees to ask themselves, including you:

- Does this culture and its values align with who you are and your values?
- What are you looking for in terms of management style, developmental opportunities, collegiality, and so on?
- Is your organization a place where you feel valued, where you feel supported, where you feel like you can do what you do best every day?

A number of years ago, the folks at Gallup did considerable research on "what great managers do differently," which led to their strengths-based leadership models, and ultimately their work on employee engagement which we've already discussed. Out of this work, they identified twelve questions for effective management.[26] They include things like "At work, do my opinions seem to count?" and "Do I know what is expected of me at work?" Allison loves to use these questions as part of the annual review process as a point of check-in with her people. But these are also great "culture fit" questions that anyone can reflect on for themselves. Try them out with your employees and see what kind of conversations they inspire. Their answers just might surprise you.

No matter what, remember that the buck stops with you. If the culture of your organization is not one that you like or that seems to inspire good work, that's on you to fix. Your words matter. Your behavior matters. The behaviors you reward and those you discipline matter. This is the work of management. Ultimately, someone has to be the grown up in the room, and that someone is you.

Questions for Reflection

- What is the culture of your organization? What are those norms and organizational values that get upheld? What gets rewarded and what doesn't?
- Where are the gaps between the stated values of the organization, and the actual lived values on a day-to-day basis? What does that mean for you, as a manager?
- Is this a place where you feel valued, where you feel supported, where you feel like you can do what you do best every day?

9. Figuring Out What's Next

As I write this, I am six months away from needing a job at the conclusion of my fellowship. If I told you that it wasn't scary to see that in writing, it would be a lie... yes, even if I *do* work for a career office. I have an idea of what will come next, which is getting clearer all the time, but it is still much of a mystery to me. I've learned that figuring out your next steps, no matter your stage of life, can be both challenging and exciting.

Depending on the day, I am faced with a wave of uncertainty, anxiety, curiosity, and frustration. I ask myself a series of questions:

- What if I don't like my next job?
- How will I pay my rent if I don't get a job as soon as this one ends?
- Should I move somewhere close by or should I live across the country?

I also have discovered a game-changer to moving through this uncertainty with some peace: take it one step at a time. This is significant because you can start this at any time; you don't need to wait until you have a huge epiphany or 3-hour long blocks on your calendar. Because, honestly, that's probably not going to happen. Instead, start now by just taking one small action towards figuring out what comes next, and then taking another one, and then taking another.

So, yes, I am six months away from needing my next job. More importantly, I have six months behind me that I have used wisely. Unlike my senior year of college, I didn't wait until time was up to think actively about the job search process. Instead, I used the first several months after graduation and in this new job – along with the self-reflection, real work experience, and introduction to new things that came along with them – to inform and further clarify my next steps.

Timing is different for everyone, and not everyone will follow the same timeline as I have. Maybe you will start a one- or two-year program, or maybe you'll begin a job that doesn't end until you decide it does. No matter your timeline, you can make use of each day to set some intentional learning goals and to reflect on what you are learning along the way.

For me, this looks like processing my workday with my friends or mentors and talking through what I liked and didn't like about my day. When I realize a part of my work fulfills a value I have, or when I realize that it doesn't, I make a note of it. I schedule informational interviews, and they often lead to insights that I write down. I try to think about what my body is telling me about my workday. Do I feel anxious? Happy? Active? Bored? Those may be fleeting emotions in the moment, but if they happen consistently, I can start to discern why when I look through the pages of my journal.

None of those activities involve drafting a cover letter or sending in a job application or making permanent decisions of any kind. Those things are important, but they have their time and place. Figuring out your next steps doesn't have to be a harrowing process of sending out mindless job applications. You can and will make progress on figuring out your next steps every day if you become actively reflective about your present routine. Discern what you want to keep the same and what you want to change, and let those reflections inform where you go next. You will figure it out. You always have, haven't you?

Advice for the New Professional

At some point during this first year, you're going to start to get a little itchy. You're going to settle into your routine, mostly figure out your job, start to find friends and a life outside of work, and you probably are going to think to yourself, *Is this all there is?* First, let's recognize that those feelings are normal. The routine of adulthood can be incredibly boring if your job is a typical 8-5. At a certain point you realize that your life is a process of getting up, going to work, coming home, making dinner, watching some TV, going to bed, and doing it all over the next day. Second, we've discussed the differences between school-life and work-life, and this is one of the biggest and worth repeating: the way that time is structured is vastly different. And you're either going to love it, or you're not.

Unless you're in a one-year fellowship experience like Katherine, or graduate school, or some other time-limited experience, we are not big fans of you jumping ship to something new after one year, unless there is a good reason for it. Allison will tell you she left her first professional experience after just a few months, without anything else lined up, because that's how toxic and miserable it was. And she doesn't regret making that choice. However, it also led to her taking temporary work at the university where she had recently completed her masters because it was incredibly difficult to find another job. Choices have consequences.

So, unless you're in one of those situations, what you don't need on your resume are a series of short-term work experiences. While the traditional structure of work is changing – no longer do people expect you to join one organization and stay there for the next forty years – there is still value in consistent, progressive work experience. And, one year just is not enough time to really understand an organization, a role, or your opportunities for growth. It takes about a year just to get a handle on the rhythm of things; when you will have busy times, when you will have slow times, what those norms and expectations are, and how to capitalize on them.

It's also important to note that while you no longer are expected to stick with one organization for the duration of your career, it's OK if you choose to do so! There is no rule that says you have to leave, just because other people are. Or that a "successful" career path is one with lots of moves in it. What's nice about this moment we're living in is that there really aren't many rules anymore. You get to determine your own career path and figure out what works for you. Of course, the challenge is in doing the work to figure that out. Without guidance or a structured career pathing process, without clear rules about how to get an "A" in life, it can be difficult to know where to begin.

So, let us show you how. It starts with four simple things which you can and should start to work on now, whether you're job searching or not.

First, you need to identify your core values. You can do a simple online search for "values list" or "core values" and you will find tons of lists you can use for this. Use these as a starting place to get your thoughts together. Ultimately, you want to come up with no more than five. What are those core beliefs or non-negotiables that guide your choices and your decisions? For example, Allison's are autonomy, creativity, family, integrity, stability.

These are the five things that shape how she thinks about her career choices and her life choices. How does your current role align with your values?

Second, identify your motivation to work. Some might call this meaning and purpose. We find these specific terms to be hard to describe and loaded with a lot of value judgment (and honestly, in your Year One, it's a pretty tall order to be able to define your meaning and purpose). Instead, we encourage you to think about your motivation to work, or why you show up every day. A number of years ago researchers identified the three core motivations or orientations to work. If you're working a job, the work is a means to an end, a way of supporting other goals or interests. If you're building a career, you are motivated by the climb, and interested in greater responsibility, promotion, and achievement. And if you're pursuing a calling, then you are motivated by mission-centered work, in whatever way that you define that.[27] The keys to these three motivations are: there is no one right motivation, it's whatever is right for you; these can and will change over time; and we all have one (or you might sit somewhere between two). What is your motivation and how does your current role align with it?

Third, we come back to goal setting, and this time it's all about you. Go back to that SMART goal model and set no more than three goals for yourself. Where do you want to be a year from now? What do you want to learn or be able to do? What are the gaps that you need to fill? You may find that some of those gaps can be filled at work, for example through stretch work assignments. But you may need to do some of this work on your own time. You may need to get a certification or other type of training. You may need to seek out a volunteer role. You may need to learn more about another industry or organization. But notice the common theme, here: You do the work.

And **fourth**, while you do the work, **remember that you don't have to do the work alone.** Once you have a good handle on your values and work orientation, your gaps and your goals, reach out to the people in your network to share the work you're doing and to seek out feedback. Network-building is relationship-building, and it's a process. That's why you want to start to do this work now, before you need to make a change, so that it will pay off down the road when you're ready to do so.

- What are your core values and how do they help you think about your work and life decisions?
- Are you motivated by working a job, building a career, or pursuing a calling? How does your current role align with that orientation?
- What goals do you need to set to get clarity on your next steps? Who can help you?

Advice for Managers

One of the worst things we do as managers is that we try to hold back good people. It happens all the time. We may not have the ability to promote someone, and instead of helping them find what's next, even if it means them leaving, we do everything that we can to keep them. Why? Because if they leave then we have to replace them, and that makes our lives difficult.

Additionally, today's young people have gotten a pretty bad reputation for jumping from one job to another when the next best opportunity comes along. Research has demonstrated that this isn't entirely true; today's young people aren't job-hopping with any greater frequency than previous generations.[28] But there's also no question that today's career paths are less linear than they used to be and built more around the individual than the organization.

The best thing you can do as a manager is to talk to your people about their career goals and their paths forward from day one. Make it clear that you expect them to advance, and to possibly move on, and that you want to be part of the process. Talk about why they come to work – what's their motivation – and how the work aligns with that *why*. Talk about the skills they want to develop and the gaps they want to fill. And then help them to think about ways to do that work.

Unfortunately, you can't always help fulfill goals for your people, even if they've done the work. You may have an employee who is eager to advance and get promoted, and they simply aren't ready and you can't give it to them. Or there may not be any promotions to give. Or, the work may not align with their goals and their motivations, but they still need to show up and do the job that's expected of them. All of this is OK. But what you don't want to have happen is your employees sneaking around having job interviews without your knowledge because they're terrified that you will find out. This happens all the time, and it's a key sign that you are managing a toxic work culture. That's not the employee's fault, it's yours, and you need to fix it.

It's also important to recognize that "advancement" means different things to different people. Kim Scott, in her book *Radical Candor*, talks about how all organizations have both rock stars and superstars.[29] The superstars are on an upward trajectory, motivated by the climb. The rock stars just want to do great work. Unfortunately, all too often we manage everyone as if they are or they should be a superstar. But you can't manage individual people the same way. And all organizations need both. Going back to Gallup, it comes down to you, as a manager, getting to know your people as individuals, with unique talents, strengths, interests, and motivations to work. It starts with a conversation.

The irony is, people want to be part of organizations where they feel supported and valued, no matter what the actual work is. Generally speaking, people don't leave jobs, they leave managers. They leave organizations that don't treat them well. So don't think, if I talk to my people about how they want to grow, it will just encourage them to leave. Think instead, if I talk to my people about how they want to grow, and support them in that, I'm just giving them an incredible reason to want to stay.

Questions for Reflection

- What do you know about your employee's career goals? What do you know about their motivation to work?
- How can you create an intentional career development plan with your employee?
- How are you creating a culture that supports individual growth and development?

Conclusion

A Final Note for the New Professional

Adulting is hard. This phrase has become a huge cliche at this point, used in reference to everything from work to paying bills to doing laundry to just generally showing up every day and taking care of one's self. It's a funny, usable quip, and there's a reason it works. Clichés become clichés because there is truth there. Becoming a fully-fledged adult is, in fact, hard. Sometimes it's not much fun. It's filled with challenges and disappointments and adjustments that no one is really prepared for when they graduate from college. And just because it's hard doesn't mean you don't have to show up and do it. There is no other option, in fact.

Adulting is hard, but it doesn't have to be terrible. In fact, just as much as you have to show up and do it, you *get* to show up and do it. You get to determine, from day one, the type of adult human you want to be out in the world. You get to choose the types of people you want to surround yourself with, how you will spend your time, how you will spend your money and other resources, and even the type of work you want to do. By changing your "have to's" to your "get to's" you get the opportunity to write your own narrative moving forward, and there is great freedom in that. It doesn't mean that it's all going to be easy or smooth sailing. It doesn't mean that the job you have now is going to be your dream job, or the place where you live now is going to be your forever home. There's a lot of work to be done in this business of being an adult. And you're just at the beginning.

We hope, through these pages, that you've gained some perspective and some insight into what you are experiencing, and perhaps a feeling that you're not alone. What you are feeling right now, what you are struggling with, what you are excited about: those are normal feelings and experiences. One of the programs we run brings together groups of young professionals to discuss their experiences and to develop strategies for navigating work and life. Every single time someone will say, "It's so nice to know that other people are going through the same things I am." There is comfort in community and in shared experiences. Find your peer group and talk about what you are going through. Use this book if it helps you.

We hope that you have reflected a bit on what you are learning about yourself, what you are looking for from work and life, and how to start to put those wants into action. We hope that your manager has learned a bit about how to be a better manager to young professionals, in general, and to you in particular. We hope that the two of you, together, have engaged in conversation about expectations and goals and success and growth. You still don't know everything, since life is a process of becoming and learning. But we hope you know more about yourself now than when you started.

We started this project as a way of sharing some of our experiences with others and to spend time in reflection and conversation with each other. We firmly believe that asking questions and listening to feedback are gifts; ones that should be given freely and honored and valued. When another person is willing to share a bit of their story with you, pay attention to that. When someone asks you for guidance, be grateful for that. Work and life and yes, adulting, is hard enough. We can all make it a little easier by moving through it with a bit more intentionality, humility, vulnerability, and gratitude.

This book was never meant to answer all your questions or to cover everyone's experiences, and we know there are a lot of both that we have left out. That was done unintentionally, but also with an awareness of the limitations of our own lived experiences and the wisdom we can share here. What we do know is this: your life – your adult life – is long, and it presents a tremendous opportunity to seek out growth, to build relationships of care, to stay curious and ask questions, to constantly be evolving and becoming. This is, after all, just your Year One. There are so many good things to come.

References

1. See, for example, University of Massachusetts, Amherst. (n.d.). *Antiracism resources*. Diversity, equity, and inclusion. Retrieved February 13, 2021, from https://www.umass.edu/diversity/ antiracism-resources; Human Rights Campaign. (n.d.). *Tools for equality and inclusion*. Resources. Retrieved February 13, 2021, from https://www.hrc.org/resources; Brown, A. C. (2018). *I'm still here: Black dignity in a world made for whiteness*. NY: Convergent; Chugh, D. (2018). *The person you mean to be: How good people fight bias*. NY: Harper Collins; Harts, M. (2019). *The memo: What women of color need to know to secure a seat at the table*. NY: Seal Press; Oluo, I. (2019). *So you want to talk about race*. NY: Seal Press.
2. The Avett Brothers. (2008). *The Gleam* [Album]. Ramseur Records.
3. William Bridges Associates. (n.d.). *Bridges transition model*. Retrieved February 13, 2021, from https://wmbridges.com/about/what-is-transition/
4. Ibid.
5. For some good resources on the topic of money see: The Financial Gym. (n.d.). Retrieved February 13, 2021, from https://financialgym.com/; Jean Chatzky. (n.d.). Retrieved February 13, 2021, from https://www.jeanchatzky.com/; Mint. (n.d.). Retrieved February 13, 2021, from https://mint.intuit.com/; Suze Orman. (n.d.). Retrieved February 13, 2021, from http://www.suzeorman.com/
6. Harter, J. (2020). 4 factors driving record-high employee engagement in U.S. *Gallup*. https://www.gallup.com/workplace/284180/factors-driving-record-high-employee-engagement.aspx
7. Novotney, A. (2019). The risks of social isolation. *Monitor on Psychology*, 50(5), 32. http://www.apa.org/monitor/2019/05/ce-corner-isolation; Offord, C. (2020). How social isolation affects the brain. *The Scientist*. https://www.the-scientist.com/features/how-social-isolation-affects-the-brain-67701; Umberson, D., & Montez, J.K. (2010). Social relationships and health: A Flashpoint for health policy. *Journal of Health and Social Behavior*, 51(1_suppl), S54–S66. https://doi.org/10.1177/0022146510383501
8. See, for example: Cohen, P., & Hsu, T. (2020, June 30). Pandemic could

scar a generation of working mothers. *The New York Times.*
https://www.nytimes.com/2020/06/03/business/economy/
coronavirus-working-women.html; Kashen, J., Glynn, S.J., & Novello,
A. (2020, October 30). *How COVID-19 sent women's workforce progress
backwards. Center for American Progress.*
https://www.americanprogress.org/issues/women/reports/2020/
10/30/492582/covid-19-sent-womens-workforce-progress-
backward/

9. Granovetter, M. S. (1973). The strength of weak ties. *American Journal of Sociology*, 78(6), 1360-1380. https://www.jstor.org/stable/2776392

10. See, for example: Cutruzzula, K. (2018, June 29). *How to build closer relationships.* TED. Retrieved February 15, 2021, from https://ideas.ted.com/how-to-build-closer-relationships/

11. Hendriksen, E. (2019, January 1). *Research shows friend groups shrink after age 25. Here's how to keep making friends even as you get older.* Insider. Retrieved February 15, 2019, from https://www.businessinsider.com/how-to-make-friends-as-an-adult-2018-10

12. Arnett, J. J. (2000). Emerging adulthood: A theory of development from the late teens through the twenties. *American Psychologist*, 55(5), 469-480. https://doi.org/10.1037/0003-066X.55.5.469

13. Hartley, C. A., & Somerville, L. H. (2015). The neuroscience of adolescent decision-making. *Current opinion in behavioral sciences*, 5, 108-115. https://doi.org/10.1016/j.cobeha.2015.09.004

14. James, G. (2019, October 23). *What goal setting does to your brain and why it's spectacularly effective.* Inc. Retrieved February 15, 2021, from https://www.inc.com/geoffrey-james/what-goal-setting-does-to-your-brain-why-its-spectacularly-effective.html; Morgan, K. (2020, July 20). *Why making plans helps manage pandemic stress.* BBC. Retrieved February 15, 2021, from https://www.bbc.com/worklife/article/20200720-how-planning-helps-us-cope-with-uncertainty

15. Cohen, J. (2020, January 12). *Reasons why we don't achieve new years resolutions.* Forbes. Retrieved February 15, 2021, from https://www.forbes.com/sites/jennifercohen/2020/01/12/reasons-why-we-dont-achieve-resolutions/

16. Sutton, R., & Wigert, B. (2019, May 6). *More harm than good: The truth about performance reviews.* Gallup. Retrieved February 15, 2021 from https://www.gallup.com/workplace/249332/harm-good-truth-

performance-reviews.aspx

17. Abrams, A. (2018, June 20). *Yes, impostor syndrome is real. Here's how to deal with it.* Time. Retrieved February 15, 2021, from https://time.com/5312483/how-to-deal-with-impostor-syndrome/; Richards, C. (2015, October 26). *Learning to deal with the impostor syndrome.* New York Times. Retrieved February 15, 2021 from https://www.nytimes.com/2015/10/26/your-money/learning-to-deal-with-the-impostor-syndrome.html

18. Opong, D. (2021, February 1). *5 steps to shake the feeling that you're an impostor.* NPR. Retrieved February 15, 2021, from https://www.npr.org/2021/01/22/959656202/5-steps-to-shake-the-feeling-that-youre-an-impostor; Weir, K. (2013). *Feel like a fraud?* gradPSYCH Magazine. Retrieved February 15, 2021, from https://www.apa.org/gradpsych/2013/11/fraud

19. See, for example, Enayati, A. (2021, June 1). *The importance of belonging.* CNN.com. Retrieved February 15, 2021, from https://www.cnn.com/2012/06/01/health/enayati-importance-of-belonging/index.html

20. Molinksy, A., & Pisman, S. (2019). The biggest hurdles recent graduates face entering the workplace. *Harvard Business Review.* https://hbr.org/2019/04/the-biggest-hurdles-recent-graduates-face-entering-the-workforce; Rikleen, L.S. (2020). What your youngest employees need most right now. *Harvard Business Review.* https://hbr.org/2020/06/what-your-youngest-employees-need-most-right-now

21. Bradberry, T., & Greaves, J. (2009). *Emotional Intelligence 2.0.* San Diego, CA: TalentSmart.

22. See, for example, Tobak, S. (2014, September 16). *Don't believe the hype around 'emotional intelligence.'* Entrepreneur. Retrieved February 15, 2021, from https://www.entrepreneur.com/article/237459

23. Bradberry, T., & Greaves, J. (2009). *Emotional Intelligence 2.0.* San Diego, CA: TalentSmart.

24. Ibid.

25. Dweck, C. (2016, January 13). *What having a 'growth mindset' actually means.* Harvard Business Review. Retrieved February 15, 2021, from https://hbr.org/2016/01/what-having-a-growth-mindset-actually-means

26. Buckingham, M. & Coffman, C. (2016). *First break all the rules: What great managers do differently.* NY: Simon & Schuster.

27. Wrzesniewski, A., McCauley, C, Rozin, P., & Schwartz, B. (1997). Jobs, Careers, and Callings: People's Relations to Their Work, *Journal of Research in Personality, 31*(1), 21-33. doi.org/10.1006/jrpe.1997.2162.

28. See, for example: Fry, R. (2017, April 19). *Millennials aren't job hopping any faster than generation x did.* Pew Research Center. Retrieved February 15, 2021, from https://www.pewresearch.org/fact-tank/2017/04/19/millennials-arent-job-hopping-any-faster-than-generation-x-did/

29. Scott, K. (2019). *Radical candor.* NY: St. Martin's Press.

Acknowledgements

Rarely does anything successful happen as a solitary pursuit, and this Year One project is no exception. Together we would like to thank the following individuals who contributed so much to these pages. Patrick Sullivan, Shan Woolard, and Mark Handler, who used their personal time to provide invaluable feedback on early drafts; your careful read and critical eye made this text so much better. Lauren Beam and Megan Hoyt, who provided feedback, support, and encouragement, and are the two best colleagues anyone could ask for. Additionally, thanks to Lauren who designed the front and back covers with her fantastic design skills. Bill Kane, who as always provided great humor and guidance through the final editing and publishing process and Celeste Holcomb, who provided line edits and great feedback on places where we could be more thoughtful about our own privilege; we quite literally could not have done this without you!

Allison: I would like to thank my colleagues at Wake Forest and especially within the Office of Personal & Career Development. You each have taught me so much about professionalism and management over the years, and you not only provide a space to take on a project such as this, but you champion it. Additionally, the Wake Forest Fellows program has taught me so much over the years about management, mentoring, and young professional development, and I am so grateful to those Wake Forest alumni and to Marybeth Wallace for continuing to invite me into the room. Finally, I would like to thank Katherine Laws for including me on her Year One journey, for listening, asking great questions, embracing learning, staying curious, and being a superstar young professional in the midst of a less-than-ideal situation. Your great humor and attitude have been a bright light during a sometimes-dark year, my friend. I'm so excited for the adventure you are about to begin, and I can't wait to see where it takes you.

Katherine: I would have none of the wisdom captured in this book, nor the confidence to write it down, without my mentors and managers in the Office of Personal and Career Development at Wake Forest University: Allison McWilliams, Andy Chan, Austin Wechter, Patrick Sullivan, and Stuart Mease. Thank you all for quieting the room to hear my voice, giving me sound wisdom, teaching me with valuable feedback, answering my questions with patience, and helping me build a purposeful career. You all have given me the highest standard for my supervisors moving forward.

Thank you to all of the members of the Wake Forest career team, especially the career coaching team, the Alumni Personal and Career Development Center, and the employer relations team for your commitment to my growth, wellbeing, and belonging even in a year where most of us never met in person. Anything good in my career to come will be because you all helped me take my first steps!

Thank you to the Wake Forest Fellows, for being the best friends with whom to share my Year One. Thank you to my roommates, for creating a home with me that serves as our office, our retreat, and our place to remember what (and who) matters. Thank you to my family, for your support and encouragement of my education, my career, and my life.

And a special thank you to Allison McWilliams, my mentor and co-author, for providing me with a safe, honest, and patient space to process all the mayhem that the Year One holds, from how to feel fulfilled in my career to how to do my job well to how to change out my smoke detector batteries. Thank you for your faithful investment in my growth that somehow both makes me feel less alone *and* empowers me to take ownership over my own life. I am grateful for all you've done in my Year One!